Backroad Bicycling
in Kentucky's Bluegrass

Backroad Bicycling
in Kentucky's Bluegrass

GEORGE GARBER

25 Rides in the
Bluegrass Region,
Lower Kentucky
Valley, Central
Heartlands, and More

THE COUNTRYMAN PRESS
WOODSTOCK, VERMONT

AN INVITATION TO THE READER Although it is unlikely that the roads you cycle on these tours will change much with time, some road signs, landmarks, and other items may. If you find that such changes have occurred on these routes, please let the author and publisher know, so that corrections may be made in future editions. Other comments and suggestions are also welcome. Address all correspondence to: Editor, Backroad Bicycling Series, The Countryman Press, P.O. Box 748, Woodstock, VT 05091.

Copyright © 2004 by George Garber

First Edition

Library of Congress Cataloging-in-Publication Data
Garber, G. (George)
    Backroad bicycling in Kentucky's bluegrass : 25 rides in the
    Bluegrass Region, Lower Kentucky Valley, Central Heartlands,
    and more / George Garber.—1st ed.
        p. cm.
    ISBN 0-88150-625-7
    1. Bicycle touring—Kentucky—Bluegrass Region—Guidebooks.
2. Bluegrass Region (Ky.)—Guidebooks. I. Title.
GV1045.5.K42B584 2004
796.6'4'097694—dc22

                                                                2004049832

Cover and interior design by Bodenweber Design
Composition by PerfecType, Nashville, TN
Cover photograph © Dennis Coello
Interior photographs by the author
Maps by Moore Creative Designs, © The Countryman Press

Published by The Countryman Press,
P.O. Box 748, Woodstock, Vermont 05091

Distributed by W. W. Norton & Company, Inc.,
500 Fifth Avenue, New York, NY 10110

Printed in the United States of America
10 9 8 7 6 5 4 3 2 1

For Dad, who introduced me to bicycles.
And for Carol, who introduced me to Kentucky.

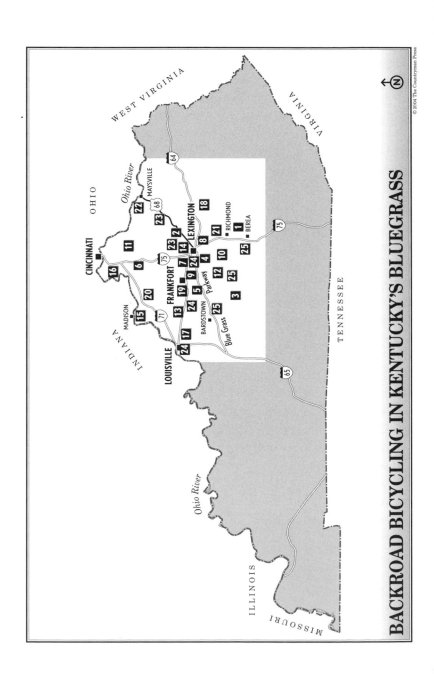

BACKROAD BICYCLING IN KENTUCKY'S BLUEGRASS

CONTENTS

ACKNOWLEDGMENTS   Some of the folks to whom I owe the most will never read this book. Ken Kifer of Alabama showed me that to tour happily you need the right attitude, not the latest equipment and the most fashionable clothes. Tragically, his bicycling days ended in 2003 when a reckless driver ran him down.

Two motorists, miles and hours apart, offered lifts when I rode the lower Kentucky Valley on a bitterly cold January day. I didn't need their help, but knowing I could have had it warmed me more than they will ever know.

The staff at Pedal Power Bike Shop in Lexington spent far more time answering my questions and helping me find oddball spare parts than my meager spending there could possibly justify.

My friend and business partner, Robert Costa, never complained about the extra work I stuck him with as riding and writing took up more and more of my time. I might have finished the book without his help, but I would have gone bankrupt.

The greatest thanks go to Carol, my wife. She encouraged me to start the book, and she pushed me to finish it. She picked most of the photographs, too. Without her input, this book would probably include 20 pictures of bridges, since I seem to be far too fond of them.

BACKROAD BICYCLE TOURS AT A GLANCE

RIDE	REGION	DISTANCE
1. Berea Bike Path	Inner Bluegrass	4.6 miles
2. Colville Bridge	Inner Bluegrass	14.0 miles
3. Perryville	Eden Shale Belt	15.4 miles
4. Lexington West	Inner Bluegrass	17.8 miles
5. Whiskey Rivers	Inner Bluegrass	18.1/21.2 mile
6. Ridges of Grant County	Eden Shale Belt	19.6 miles
7. Horse Farms West	Inner Bluegrass	22.2 miles
8. Lexington East	Inner Bluegrass	22.3/26.9 mile
9. The Asparagus Patch	Inner Bluegrass	22.7 miles
10. Camp Nelson	Inner Bluegrass	23.0 miles
11. Licking River	Eden Shale Belt	26.5 miles
12. High Bridge	Inner Bluegrass	28.2 miles
13. Shelby County	Outer Bluegrass	29.4 miles

BIKE	DIFFICULTY	HIGHLIGHTS
Road	Easy	Kentucky's arts-and-crafts capital
Road	Easy	A pleasant ride to a covered bridge
Road	Moderate	Civil War battlefield
Road	Moderate	Farmland just past the city limits
Hybrid	Strenuous	Bourbon distilleries, a remote dirt road, and a ford across the Salt River
Road	Moderate	Ridgetop views and quiet roads
Road	Moderate	Horse country and Keeneland Race Course
Road	Strenuous	Foxhunting country and a very steep hill
Road	Moderate	A thrilling descent into the Kentucky River Gorge
Hybrid	Strenuous	Remote roads and Kentucky River bridges
Hybrid	Moderate	River views
Road	Moderate	Kentucky River Gorge
Hybrid	Moderate	Jeptha Knob, the highest point in the Bluegrass

RIDE	REGION	DISTANCE
14. Horse Farms East	Inner Bluegrass	31.9 miles
15. Ohio River Valley	Outer Bluegrass	33.3 miles
16. Big Bones	Outer Bluegrass	34.6 miles
17. Floyds Fork Valley	Outer Bluegrass	37.7 miles
18. Pilot Knob	Eden Shale Belt	41.1/44.6 mile
19. Big Roads	Inner Bluegrass	47.7 miles
20. Lower Kentucky Valley	Outer Bluegrass	47.8 miles
21. Following Daniel Boone	Inner Bluegrass	49.4 miles
22. Old Man River	Outer Bluegrass	49.8 miles
23. Lexington to Blue Licks	Entire Bluegrass region	52.9 miles
24. Louisville to Lexington	Entire Bluegrass region	71.8 miles
25. The TransAmerica Trail	Entire Bluegrass region	99.6 miles

BIKE	DIFFICULTY	HIGHLIGHTS
Road	Moderate	Horse country
Road	Moderate	Old river ports
Road	Moderate	Fossils of mammoths trapped at salt lick
Road	Moderate	Rural valley near Louisville
Hybrid	Moderate	Hill from which Daniel Boone first saw the Bluegrass region
Road	Easy	The Capitol, the Vietnam Veterans' Memorial, and wide, paved shoulders
Road	Moderate	Port towns and river views
Road	Moderate	Daniel Boone's first settlement
Road	Moderate	Ohio River views, covered bridges, and Underground Railroad sites
Road	Strenuous	Revolutionary War battlefield
Road	Strenuous	The scenic route between Kentucky's two biggest cities
Road	Strenuous	Part of a great transcontinental bike route; three state parks

INTRODUCTION   Everybody knows the Kentucky Bluegrass. It's the land of picture-perfect horse farms, where sleek thorough-breds graze in lush fields behind miles of curving plank fences.

For once the conventional view is accurate—the horse farms are still there, and they're still magnificent—but it's incomplete. The Bluegrass is more than horse farms. It's the Kentucky River shrouded in morning mist at the bottom of its rocky gorge. It's a campground on the spot where Daniel Boone built his fort. It's a narrow road curving along a ridge with steep valleys on both sides. It's a country store with creaky wood floors and an owner who greets his customers by name.

Best of all, from the cyclist's point of view, the Bluegrass offers miles of country roads with smooth pavement (usually), light traf-fic, and some of the world's best scenery. It's a settled country—more farm than forest—and that means you are never far from a cold drink or a hot meal, or help if you need it. But it's far from crowded. You'll encounter few vehicles beyond the main urban areas, and there are only three of them: Lexington, Louisville, and suburban Cincinnati. Most people you meet will be locals, not tourists. If you've ever ridden through some of America's other famous landscapes, like Martha's Vineyard or the Napa Valley, you will be amazed at how un-touristy the Bluegrass is.

Tourists on bikes are particularly rare. On many rides you won't see another cyclist. If you love to meet other riders when you tour, you may be put off by their absence here. On the other hand, you may find it refreshing. Sure, it's fun to compare notes with fellow bicyclists. But it's also fun to ride through "virgin" territory where such riders are rare. You'll probably meet people who are fascinated, even amazed, at what you are doing.

Of course, some will think you're nuts, but they're usually too polite to say so.

WHAT'S SO BLUE ABOUT IT? The region is named for Kentucky bluegrass, which is grown in pastures and lawns. Is it really blue? Well, no. It's green, going on brown when the weather turns cold or dry. No one knows why it's called "bluegrass," but every Kentuckian has an opinion. Some people claim it actually does appear blue at certain times of the year. They never catch it on film, though. According to one story, it was named for Canadian bluegrass, a close relative that really is blue, or at least bluish.

Whatever its color, bluegrass grows well in central Kentucky, and its name has been appropriated by the region, as well as the entire state of Kentucky. Then there's bluegrass music, though that has no connection with the area. Bluegrass music originated in western Kentucky, far from the region covered in this book.

GEOLOGY Though named for a plant, the Bluegrass region is defined by geology. Its dominant feature is a thick bed of limestone that was formed at the bottom of a shallow sea between 440 and 475 million years ago. As the limestone rose above sea level, rivers and streams cut into it, creating the landscape we see today.

Limestone continues to dominate the region. You see it right out in the open at road cuts and streambeds. Even where you can't see it, limestone lies just below the surface and continues to exert its influence here. Much of the Bluegrass is riddled with sinks, springs, and caves—all characteristic of limestone country, where flowing water slowly dissolves the rock. (A sink is a bowl-like depression from which water drains into the ground rather than into a surface stream or creek.) Most of the soil was formed from limestone and is very fertile. Some folks say the limestone soil, which is rich in phosphates and other nutrients, helps explain why horses do so well here.

Geology divides the Bluegrass into three subregions. The Inner Bluegrass, which includes Lexington and nearby counties, is characterized by gentle slopes, rounded hills and valleys, and very rich soil. The famous horse farms are all located here.

The Eden Shale Belt, also called the Hills of the Bluegrass, surrounds the Inner Bluegrass in a ring up to 30 miles wide. It has steeper slopes and V-shaped valleys, with less fertile soil. Farms here tend to look poorer and rougher than those in the Inner Bluegrass, and more land is forested.

Beyond the Eden Shale Belt lies the Outer Bluegrass, which looks a lot like the Inner Bluegrass, though with less fertile soil.

The Bluegrass is bounded on the east, south, and west by the Knobs, a geologic region defined by short, steep hills topped with sandstone. The Ohio River forms the northern boundary of the Kentucky Bluegrass, but the region doesn't really end there. It spills over to the north side of the river, where it's called the Ohio Bluegrass. (Ride 22: Old Man River goes there.)

Two great rivers cut deeply into the Bluegrass plain. The Ohio River skirts the region's northern edge, while the Kentucky River slices right through the middle. The Ohio is a far larger river, but the Kentucky has created a more spectacular valley. Near Lexington, the Kentucky River flows through a narrow gorge beneath limestone cliffs that soar 400 feet high. The gorge looks almost impossibly thin and long from the air—like an artificial groove cut into the landscape. Tributary creeks tumble down to the river in their own small gorges.

HISTORY Every story about Kentucky gets around to Daniel Boone sooner or later, so we might as well start there.

Boone didn't discover the Bluegrass region. Countless Native Americans and a handful of Europeans got there first. But Boone deserves his fame, because his arrival marked the real beginning of Anglo-American settlement in this part of America.

He reached the Bluegrass in 1769 after traveling through the densely wooded mountains of Eastern Kentucky. A few miles southeast of present-day Winchester he and his companions climbed a steep hill—probably what we call Pilot Knob these days. From the top of that rocky hill they got their first glimpse of a different landscape; a rolling savanna of scattered trees and cane fields replaced the wild forests and steep mountains they had just traversed.

This was the land Boone had been looking for. He returned here in 1775, blazing a trail up from Cumberland Gap and founding the town of Boonesborough. At about the same time another group established Harrodsburg.

Settlement proceeded with amazing speed. Thousands of people walked in through Cumberland Gap, following Boone's trail. Others floated down on the Ohio River. By the 1780s the towns of Lexington, Louisville, Maysville (then called Limestone), and Danville had all appeared on the map. Residents met to consider independence from Virginia in 1784, and eight years later Kentucky entered the Union as the 15th state. It was the first state in

The Bluegrass region is host to some beautiful horse farms.

what was then "the West"—west of the Appalachian Mountains, that is.

Over the next two centuries Lexington and Louisville grew into major cities, and Cincinnati's suburbs spilled over into the counties of the far northern Bluegrass. But the region's character remains rural, rooted in horses, tobacco, and the making of bourbon whiskey.

CYCLING CONDITIONS   If you ride in the Northeast or the Midwest, Bluegrass cycling conditions will hold few surprises for you. But if you're coming from the West or the South, you may have to get used to a thing or two. The terrain here varies greatly but has few extremes. You'll find no mountains and no extensive flatlands.

Textbooks and encyclopedias like to describe the Bluegrass as a rolling plain. That sounds nice, though those are not the words you will use to describe it when you're crawling up a 10 percent grade in your lowest gear. For a so-called plain the Bluegrass has some pretty wicked hills.

What makes the steep grades bearable, even fun, is that most are very short. The only sustained climbs occur near the big river valleys. So if your route touches the Kentucky or Ohio River, expect a long, hard pull. Elsewhere, you will have little to worry about in this regard.

Weather varies more than the terrain. Kentuckians talk like southerners, but their climate is midwestern. Winters are cold, summers are hot, and rain can fall any day of the year.

In July, the hottest month, the average daily high is 86 degrees, and the low, 66. The corresponding figures for January are 40 and 24. The all-time high is 103 degrees, and the all-time low, -21. These numbers were recorded in Lexington, but they are typical of the whole region.

Rainfall averages about 45 inches annually and is well distributed throughout the year. That is what keeps the bluegrass green. But it's not as bad as it sound. Well over half the days here are rain-free. The average number of days with no appreciable precipitation ranges from 23 in October to 17 in February.

It's possible to restrict your riding to days when the chance of rain is near zero, but you miss a lot that way. Rain isn't a big deal when you're prepared for it. On a hot summer day, a shower can be downright welcome. Even cold rain is tolerable if you wear (or pack) the right clothes.

Most local cyclists put their bikes away for the winter months, but that has more to do with custom than necessity. Snow falls in the Bluegrass—over a foot a year, on average—but it rarely sticks around. Even January and February produce some good riding days each year, and it's a shame to let them pass by. Be careful, though, and remember that country roads may retain ice and snow a day or two after the city streets have been cleaned up.

The prevailing wind blows from the south in all seasons, but it isn't consistent enough for you to plan trips around. Assume that the wind will come from any point of the compass during a ride. It's usually light—under 10 mph. On those few days when conditions are tougher, consider changing the direction of your ride so the home stretch is downwind.

Most of the tours in this book stay on paved roads. A few venture onto gravel or dirt for short distances. Even minor farm roads are paved in most Bluegrass counties, and maintenance is generally good. As you go farther out into the country, the roads tend to get narrower but generally remain hard-surfaced. You may encounter broken or rough pavement in remote areas, and washouts are sometimes patched with gravel. This can create more dangerous conditions than a normal gravel road, because you won't be expecting it.

If you are looking for rugged trails on which to test your new full-suspension mountain bike, I'm sad to say you won't find many here. Kentucky has some great trails, but the best are found in the eastern mountains. To see the Bluegrass, you must ride the roads.

Though the tours in this book don't include any mountain-bike trails, two of the rides do pass through areas where such trails exist. Ride 20 starts and ends at General Butler State Park, which has well-regarded trails and even hosts competitions. Ride 24 runs through Taylorsville Lake State Park, which has several miles of multiuse trails.

You can expect to share Bluegrass roads with cars and the occasional truck or school bus. Bike lanes are unknown outside the cities, and even there they are rare. A few highways boast paved shoulders, but cyclists and motorists must share lanes on most roads.

To cycle the Bluegrass safely, you need to know how to ride narrow roads. The keys are visibility, predictability, and willingness to take the lane. The first two are easy. To be visible, wear bright colors during the day and never ride at night without lights and reflectors. To be predictable, steer straight when you mean to go straight, clearly signal when you mean to go left or right, and obey the rules of the road.

Taking the lane is the part some people have trouble with. Cyclists are told to ride on the right, and that is good advice—but only to a point. If you always ride on the far right edge of the road, you're asking for trouble because motorists assume they can squeeze by you while staying in their own lane. Most of the time they get away with this, but sometimes they don't, and then you either get hit or are forced off the road. This is not a choice you want to face. It's better to ride farther left, which forces drivers to wait till they can pass safely. And if a vehicle does come too close, you have room to veer right without running off the road.

If you are not yet comfortable sharing lanes—or if you just hate to do it—two of the tours described in this book will be perfect for you. Ride 19 stays on roads with wide, paved shoulders for all but the last 2 miles, and you can avoid that last bit if you turn around at the Vietnam Veterans' Memorial. And except for a couple of blocks on city streets, Ride 1 stays on a bike path for its entire length.

On the more remote roads, dogs may cause you more trouble than traffic. Cross-country cyclists have reported more bike-chasing dogs in Kentucky than in any other state. I've found that the problem varies with the landscape. You rarely encounter bad dogs in the well-groomed horse country of the Inner Bluegrass. I suspect the horse owners won't put up with them. Dogs are also rare in the more remote, wooded parts of the Bluegrass. But between those extremes, you need to keep your eyes and ears open. The

real risk isn't a bite—though that's no joke—but a crash if the dog
gets under your wheels.

Even experienced cyclists differ on how best to deal with dogs.
Some riders carry chemical sprays, but I've never felt the need for
them. My approach is to outrun dogs when I can, but that only
works if the dog is slow or I'm heading downhill. When I can't outrun the dog I slow down and talk to it—gently if the dog seems
even a little bit friendly, or with a sharp "go home!" if it seems
aggressive. This almost always works, often converting a chaser
into a tail-wagging friend. If the dog keeps coming, I stop and dismount. If I ever have to fight off a dog, I want to be on my feet.
But thankfully it has never gone that far.

Kentucky law treats bicycles the same as other vehicles, with
very few exceptions. Bikes are allowed on all roads except limited-
access highways. In the Bluegrass, the only restricted highways
are the interstates, the Blue Grass and Mountain Parkways, and
the west half of New Circle Road in Lexington. You can ride on
the road shoulder (where it exists), but you don't have to. Helmets
are not required, except on certain off-road trails. If you ride after
dark the law requires that you have a white light in front and a
red reflector or light in back. The police, and many cyclists, ignore
that law, but I urge you to obey it if you want to stay alive.

THE TOURS   This book includes 25 tours that range from 5 easy
miles on a small-town bike path to 100 hilly miles on the Trans-
America Trail. You can go even farther on Ride 23: Lexington to
Blue Licks if you make it a round trip.

Are these the absolute best rides in the Bluegrass? It depends,
because cyclists differ in what they consider a good ride. Some riders seek an athletic challenge. For them, a good ride goes on and
on and climbs punishing grades. Other riders demand the lightest
possible traffic. One group might favor smooth pavement, while
another delights in negotiating rock-strewn dirt roads. I prefer
good scenery and an interesting destination, and I don't mind busy
highways or muddy roads if they take me where I want to go.

But it's not all about me, so this isn't simply a list of my
favorite rides. I've tried to include a variety of tours, along with

It's possible to bike the Bluegrass year-round. Here the author takes a break on a trip into the Kentucky River Gorge.

enough descriptive information that you can decide which ones best suit you. You may not love them all, but you should be able to find a few terrific rides here no matter what style of biking you prefer.

And don't be afraid to try a ride that falls outside your normal pattern. It might surprise you. For example, my attitude toward bike paths used to border on contempt. But in scouting rides for this book I tried the Beebe-White Bike Path in Berea. I liked it so much that I have included it here (see Ride 1).

Most of the tours are loops, because such rides are easy to organize and don't cover the same ground twice. The only one-way rides described here are long cross-country routes.

The starting points all have easy car parking (except for Ride 24) because I assume that most riders will arrive in a motor vehicle.

But please don't think that is the only way. If you live in Lexington or are a visitor who is based there, you can bike to many of the starting points. Consult a city map—the phone book has one—and head out.

The local bus is a good choice if you really hate riding in city traffic. Every bus in Lexington has a front rack that can carry two bikes. Louisville buses also accept bikes, but you need to call a day ahead to make sure the bus you'll be taking will have a rack. You can reach Rides 4, 7, 8, 14, 17, 21, and 24 by bus. The bus stop is often not the official starting point, but it's always on the route or within an easy ride of it. For bus information in Lexington, call 859-253-4636; in Louisville, call 502-585-1234.

The tours are listed by length, from short to long. Every tour except Ride 1 has its share of hills, so you can assume difficulty is roughly proportional to length.

GETTING TO THE BLUEGRASS Most visitors to the area arrive by car, but planes, trains, and buses can also do the job. Greyhound buses cross the Bluegrass on three routes, following I-75, I-71, and I-64. Buses stop in the towns of Louisville, Carrollton, Frankfort, Lexington, Mount Sterling, Richmond, and Berea. Your bike must be boxed, but there is no extra charge if the dimensions—length plus width plus height—don't exceed 62 inches.

One Amtrak train, the Cardinal, grazes the northeast edge of the Bluegrass and stops at Maysville. This train—though not all Amtrak trains—accepts roll-on bikes for a $15 fee. You don't need a box.

Air travelers can choose from three airports: Louisville, Lexington, and Cincinnati (which is really in Kentucky, and not far from Ride 16). Airlines are a lot less hospitable than Greyhound and Amtrak about lugging bikes aboard. Most charge a hefty fee ($75 to $100) and require that you box your bike.

Unless you have a special reason to prefer one of the others, Lexington's airport, Bluegrass Field, is your best bet. It's located right in the heart of the Inner Bluegrass horse country and is very easy to bike in and out of. I've occasionally popped into the airport just to fill my water bottle. I bet nobody does that at LaGuardia or O'Hare.

Calumet Farm entrance.

EQUIPMENT You can ride any kind of bike on these tours, but some types work better than others. Most Bluegrass roads are smooth enough for road bikes with skinny tires, and that's the ride of choice for many locals. I prefer a touring bike, which has the dropped handlebars of a road bike but includes details that make it better for long rides and imperfect roads. Compared to a road bike, a touring model has a longer wheelbase, lower gears, and wider tires. It usually has luggage racks, but you can fit racks to other kinds of bikes, too.

A mountain bike will also get the job done, and might come in handy on Rides 5 and 13. On the longer tours, you may find that a mountain bike's wide tires slow you down. If a mountain bike happens to be your favorite (or only) mount, consider switching to thinner road tires for your Bluegrass rides.

Gearing is a matter of personal preference, but remember that almost every tour includes a few steep hills. Too low always beats not low enough. My bottom gear is 29 inches, and it seems I use it at least once on every long ride. If you are younger and stronger than I (and most people are), you may be able to get away with a higher low gear.

Rain will be a lot easier to deal with if your bike has fenders. I confess that mine does not, but I sometimes wish it did.

You'll need to carry luggage on the longest tours unless you have someone following along in a car. Options include rear racks, front racks, and saddlebags. I even use bags on short rides because I like to carry a camera, food, and extra clothes. But many riders get by without all that stuff.

Some cyclists develop a keen interest (some might call it obsession) with their machines. They pore over bike catalogs and know all the latest products. And there's nothing wrong with that. But if you have read this far, I'm guessing you like bikes mainly for where they can take you. If you have a bike—any bike—and the chain stays on and the tires hold air, you can ride the Bluegrass. Get out and do it.

THE TOURS

Berea Bike Path

- ■ **DISTANCE:** 4.6 miles
- ■ **HIGHLIGHTS:** The Artisan Center, craft shops in downtown Berea, and easy riding

This short ride is the only one in the book that stays primarily on a bike path. People who don't ride bikes usually assume that cyclists love bike paths, but it's not that simple. Some cyclists do love bike paths and won't ride anywhere else. Others dislike bike paths intensely and avoid them at all costs. Many cyclists fall in between; they like some bike paths and dislike others.

If you favor bike paths because you think they're safer than roads, you may be making a mistake. Bike paths isolate you from the cars going your way, but they do nothing about all the cars that cross your path at intersections and driveways. Most car/bike crashes occur at those crossing points, not between vehicles headed the same way. Also, bike paths are often used by walkers, runners, and skaters, all of whom increase the risk of accidents.

So why did I include this bike-path tour in the book? Some bike paths are better than others, and this is one of the good ones. It is well designed, it doesn't cross a lot of busy streets, and it goes somewhere interesting. That last part is important. Many bike paths—including some in Lexington and Louisville—are located where they were easy to build, not where anyone would actually want to ride.

Even if bike paths are no safer than roads (and the jury is still out on that one), beginners often feel more comfortable on paths,

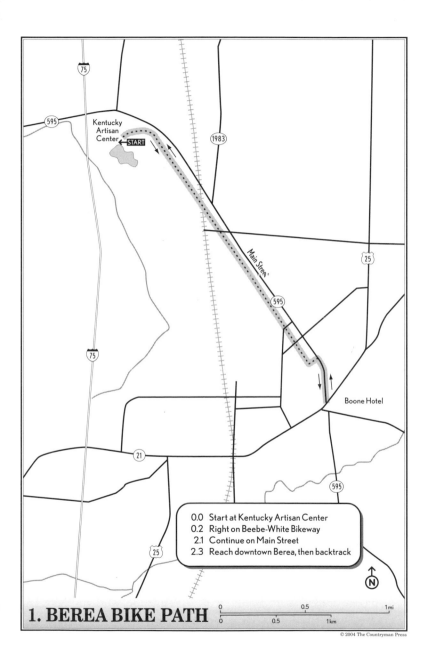

0.0 Start at Kentucky Artisan Center
0.2 Right on Beebe-White Bikeway
2.1 Continue on Main Street
2.3 Reach downtown Berea, then backtrack

1. BEREA BIKE PATH

0   0.5   1mi
0   0.5   1km

and there's nothing wrong with that. Every cyclist was a beginner once. And even if you're an experienced rider, you may have friends who don't ride but would like to try it. Berea's bike path is a good place to get them started. After a few laps here, they will be itching to join you on a country road.

Berea has been a unique Bluegrass town since its early days, but what makes it unique has changed over the years. Nineteenth-century Berea was notable for its liberal views on race. The town was founded in the 1850s by abolitionist preacher John Fee. He started a church and school for people opposed to slavery.

Abolitionists were none too popular in central Kentucky in those days, and in 1859 a mob from Richmond ran Fee out of town. He came back after the Civil War, inviting African Americans to settle in Berea and welcoming them into his church and school, which became Berea College. By 1900 blacks made up about a fourth of Berea's population and served on the town council. At that time, Berea College was the only school in Kentucky—and possibly the only school in the entire South—where whites and blacks studied together.

Berea's era of racial integration barely lasted into the 20th century, however. Most white Kentuckians, it seems, could not abide an interracial school anywhere in the state. A 1904 law forced Berea College to segregate. The college's leaders set up a separate school in Shelbyville for blacks, and Berea College became all white.

The college changed focus after that, devoting itself to educating the poor whites of Appalachia, who worked in college workshops in exchange for free tuition. Thanks in part to those workshops, Berea became known for high-quality crafts.

Today, of course, all races are again welcome at Berea College, but the current proportion of black students doesn't rival 19th-century levels. Present-day Berea is still known for its crafts, and for its college, where low-income students continue to work 10 to 15 hours a week instead of paying tuition.

Don't get the wrong idea about Berea crafts, though. Much of what passes for crafts these days at flea markets and similar venues is worthless junk that our grandparents wouldn't have allowed in the house. That's not what they make in Berea. Here you can find turned wooden bowls, fine furniture, musical instruments, and other high-quality items that represent the best work human hands can do. Some of it costs a lot, but you probably expected that.

DIRECTIONS FOR THE RIDE

This ride starts at the Kentucky Artisan Center, which provides a good introduction to the local crafts scene. It then heads to downtown Berea, where you will find crafts shops and several good restaurants.

0.0 From the bike rack in front of the Kentucky Artisan Center, head down the driveway.
The Artisan Center lies north of Berea, at Exit 77 on I-75. There is a restaurant here.

0.2 Right on Beebe–White Bikeway just before the driveway reaches KY 595.

0.8 Cross railroad tracks. A barrier forces riders to slow down here.

1.7 Pass Berea Community Elementary School.
This just may be the strangest-looking school building in Kentucky. Berea's public schools have long had a close and productive relationship with the local college, but that may be changing. For years local residents have been able to attend Berea College (provided they met the academic entry requirements) no matter how rich their families were. In contrast, applicants from elsewhere had to demonstrate financial need. The college recently decided to apply the income limits to town residents, too. It's a hot issue in Berea.

2.1 Leave the bike path, which ends here. Continue on Main Street.

2.3 Reach downtown Berea. Retrace your route to the Artisan Center for a total trip length of 4.6 miles.
The college campus is to your right in downtown Berea. Stores and restaurants line the left side of the street. A block off Main Street you'll find the Log House, which sells student-made crafts and includes a small furniture museum. It has rest rooms, too. Berea has several good eateries, but the most distinctive is the restaurant at the Boone Hotel, owned by the college and staffed by student workers.

Bicycle Shops

The nearest is in Danville.

Lodging

Stay at the Boone Hotel (859-985-3700) downtown, or try the Days Inn (859-986-7373) or Holiday Inn Express (859-985-1901) near the Kentucky Artisan Center. Berea has two commercial campgrounds: the Old Kentucky RV Park (859-986-1150) and the Walnut Meadow Campground (859-986-6180). Both are located west of town.

Colville Bridge

- **DISTANCE:** 14.0 miles
- **HIGHLIGHTS:** The Colville covered bridge and the town of Millersburg

Kentucky once had over 400 covered bridges. Today just 13 remain standing. The Inner Bluegrass has two: Switzer Bridge near Frankfort and Colville Bridge near Millersburg.

The Switzer Bridge gets most of the attention. But if I had to choose between them, I'd favor the Colville because it's still in use. A bridge that is closed to traffic, as the Switzer has been for years, is a museum piece. It's worth a look, but it doesn't satisfy like a bridge that earns its keep. The Colville Bridge still carries cars, farm trucks, and cyclists—including you, if you take this tour.

The bridge is 120 feet long—the same length as the Switzer Bridge—and dates from 1877. They say a local judge used to sentence minor criminals to paint it. That may explain why the bridge looks so good today, though surely it has had its share of professional maintenance, too.

DIRECTIONS FOR THE RIDE

The tour begins and ends in Millersburg. It's the second biggest town in Bourbon County, but that's not saying much since the county is so rural. The town has about 1,000 residents.

0.0 Start at a town park in Millersburg.

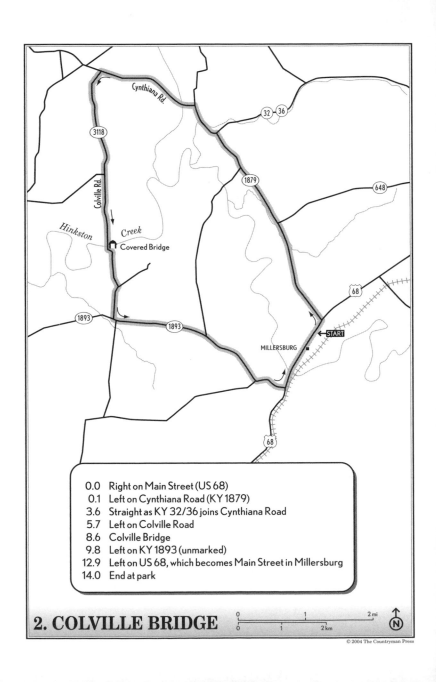

0.0	Right on Main Street (US 68)
0.1	Left on Cynthiana Road (KY 1879)
3.6	Straight as KY 32/36 joins Cynthiana Road
5.7	Left on Colville Road
8.6	Colville Bridge
9.8	Left on KY 1893 (unmarked)
12.9	Left on US 68, which becomes Main Street in Millersburg
14.0	End at park

2. COLVILLE BRIDGE

The Colville covered bridge.

The park has a narrow entrance that is easy to miss. Enter the park from Main Street (US 68) about a block northwest of the Millersburg Military Academy. Park next to the small building, which is actually Millersburg's police station. The park has picnic tables but no toilets.

0.1 Right on Main Street (US 68) as you leave the park, then left on Cynthiana Road (KY 1879).
A convenience store is located at the corner.

0.8 Stay on Cynthiana Road as Headquarters Road (KY 648) comes in from the right. Our road jogs left, then right at the junction.
The creek on the left contains an unusually good example of a water gate. Water gates are common throughout the Bluegrass, though they are unheard of in some parts of the country. A water gate carries a fence across a creek without blocking the water flow. When the water is low, the gate hangs down and keeps livestock in or out. When the water is high, the gate swings out and lets the water through with

all the floating debris. That's the idea, anyway. Water gates deteriorate fast, and many don't work. But this one looks perfect.

3.6 Straight as KY 32/36 joins Cynthiana Road.

5.7 Left on Colville Road, a one-lane road.

8.6 Reach Colville Bridge.
The bridge crosses Hinkston Creek, a major tributary of the Licking River.

9.8 Left on KY 1893 (unmarked).

12.9 Left on US 68, which becomes Main Street as it enters Millersburg.

13.0 Pass a convenience store and cross Hinkston Creek.

13.3 Enter downtown Millersburg.
There is a small grocery store and a pizzeria here.

13.9 Pass the Millersburg Military Institute.
Kentucky's only military school, it began in 1893 at another site in town.

14.0 Right into park driveway to end the ride.

Bicycle Shops

None closer than Lexington.

3

Perryville

- **DISTANCE:** 15.4 miles
- **HIGHLIGHTS:** The Perryville battlefield and old Merchants' Row in town

The Battle of Perryville was the biggest Civil War battle on Kentucky soil. Seventy-four thousand men fought here, and 1,355 died.

The fight began in August 1862 with a Confederate plan to invade Kentucky, which was then firmly in Union hands. Twenty thousand Confederates came up from Knoxville to capture most of the Inner Bluegrass, including Lexington. An even bigger Confederate force marched from Chattanooga to take Munfordville, which lies west of the Bluegrass. The goal was to lure the Union forces north from Tennessee into Kentucky, where they would—according to the Confederate plan—be defeated. That would leave Kentucky under Confederate control and might even end the war, with the South victorious.

That was the plan, anyway. But as soldiers say, war plans rarely survive contact with the enemy. Contact came on October 8, 1862, in the hills near Perryville. Incredibly, both commanding generals appear to have greatly misjudged the size of the opposing force. Thinking he was facing both Confederate armies (the one that had taken Lexington, as well as the one that had taken Munfordville), Union leader Don Carlos Buell sent three corps—58,000 troops—

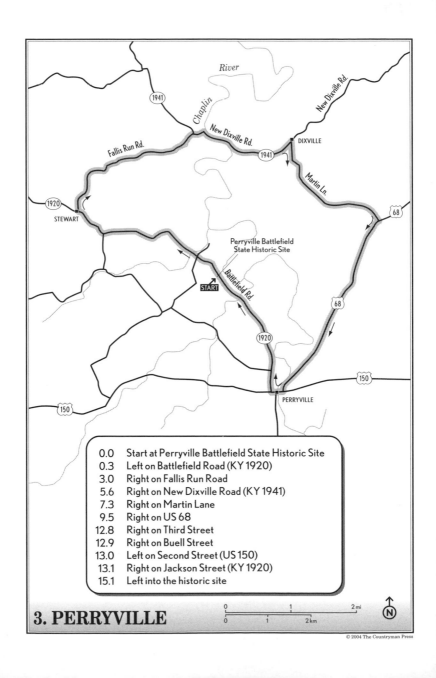

0.0	Start at Perryville Battlefield State Historic Site
0.3	Left on Battlefield Road (KY 1920)
3.0	Right on Fallis Run Road
5.6	Right on New Dixville Road (KY 1941)
7.3	Right on Martin Lane
9.5	Right on US 68
12.8	Right on Third Street
12.9	Right on Buell Street
13.0	Left on Second Street (US 150)
13.1	Right on Jackson Street (KY 1920)
15.1	Left into the historic site

3. PERRYVILLE

into battle. But only one Confederate force was in the area, with just 16,000 men.

Confederate leader Braxton Bragg believed he was facing just one Union corps instead of three. That mistake led him to order a suicidal attack that he might well have backed away from had he known what he was up against.

With such a lopsided fight, a Union win might have seemed inevitable. The Confederates did well, however, and by some accounts they scored a tactical victory. Still, that wasn't good enough, since the success of their plan required that they conquer Kentucky, not just win a battle. Now knowing how big a force he faced, Bragg fell back to Harrodsburg and eventually all the way back to Tennessee. That ended the Kentucky campaign and any serious threat to Union control over the state.

Kentucky never seceded from the Union, and most Kentuckians who fought in the war did so on the northern side, with Union enlistments outnumbering Confederate five to two. Despite that fact, you can still spot Confederate flags around Perryville and elsewhere in the Bluegrass.

And when you meet a Civil War fan in Kentucky, he (I say "he" because I have yet to meet one who wasn't male) is most likely interested in the southern side. One reason for this discrepancy is that Kentucky became more southern as the war went on, and even after it ended. Some federal officials treated Kentucky more like conquered territory than a loyal state, which pushed local sympathies farther toward the southern cause. On top of that, ex-Confederates from the Deep South moved into Kentucky after the war, bringing their attitudes and political views with them.

The tour begins at the Perryville Battlefield State Historic Site, which offers a small museum, rest rooms, and picnic tables. Memorials have been erected to the warriors on both sides. Walking trails wind through the battlefield, with signs explaining what happened.

Civil War reenactors throng here every fall, on the weekend nearest October 8. This is a good time to visit if you want to see what the battle was like—minus the death and dismemberment.

It's probably a good time to stay away if you just want a quiet ride in the country.

A good way to spend the day is to ride the tour in the morning, eat a picnic lunch at the battlefield, and then walk the battlefield trails in the afternoon. Allow an hour for the walk, more if you like to read every word on every sign.

DIRECTIONS FOR THE RIDE

Start at Perryville Battlefield State Historic Site, located in Boyle County about 12 miles west of Danville. Park near the museum.

0.0 Head down the main road from the parking lot.

0.3 Left on Battlefield Road (KY 1920) as you leave the historic site.

3.0 Right on Fallis Run Road. A long-closed country store at the corner blocks the road sign till the last minute.
From here to mile 9.5 you ride a series of paved roads that are one and a half lanes wide. This is wide enough for a bike and a car to pass without crowding each other. But when two cars pass, both drivers must squeeze over.

5.6 Right on New Dixville Road (KY 1941).
Within a mile or two you can see what's old and new in animal husbandry. What's old is chickens—but not just any chickens. You'll see yards full of roosters, each tied to its own little house, and those birds aren't for eating. They're fighting chickens. In the Bluegrass, cockfighting has a tradition that goes back as far as horseracing. Kentucky law still tolerates the sport, which most states have banned. However, gambling on the outcome is prohibited. And that is the rub, since gambling is the whole point.

What's new is goats—big Boer goats with floppy ears. Kentuckians have never eaten much goat meat, but in recent years immigrants from Mexico and the Middle East have created a market for it. Some farmers hope Boer goats can replace declining tobacco as a cash crop. The animals are bigger and meatier than the usual American goats, which were raised as much for milk as meat.

5.9 Cross the Chaplin River.
Though small, this stream played a role in the Battle of Perryville. The summer of 1862 brought terrible drought to Kentucky. Both armies needed water, but many area creeks had dried up. The Chaplin Valley still contained pools of water,

Boer goats have a growing role in Kentucky agriculture.

however, and soldiers fought over access to them throughout the day before the big battle.

For the next half mile the road climbs out of the Chaplin Valley, providing good views of the river and narrow floodplain.

7.3 Right on Martin Lane.

9.5 Right on US 68.
After miles on narrow back roads, you are now riding on a two-lane highway with no paved shoulder. It's not really a busy road, but it may seem like one after the country lanes you've just traveled over.

11.7 Pass the sign marking Perryville, though the actual town is still almost a mile ahead.
The sign claims Perryville was settled in 1770, but that is a matter of some debate. Most historians consider Harrodsburg the earliest Anglo-American settlement in Kentucky, and it dates from 1774. If settlers actually did live here as early as 1770,

they didn't call their home Perryville. The town was named for Oliver Hazard Perry, who defeated the British navy on Lake Erie in the War of 1812.

As you approach the town, the highway becomes Bragg Street, named for the Confederate general at the big battle. But Perryville plays no favorites. You'll soon encounter Buell Street, named for the Union general.

12.7 Cross Second Street and enter Perryville.
You'll find a convenience store here.

12.8 Right on Third Street.

12.8 Stop at the Chaplin River and walk your bike over the bridge.

12.9 Right on Buell Street.
Before making the turn, you may want to park and explore the neighborhood on foot. To your left are the old commercial buildings of Merchants' Row. To your right are two big plaques that further explain the battle.

13.0 Left on Second Street (US 150).

13.1 Right on Jackson Street (KY 1920).

15.1 Left into the historic site.

15.4 End at the parking lot near the museum.

Bicycle Shops

Danville Bike and Fitness, 417 West Main Street, Danville; 859-238-7669

Lodging

Danville and Harrodsburg have motels.

4

Lexington West

- **DISTANCE:** 17.8 miles
- **HIGHLIGHTS:** Picturesque rural countryside

This tour starts in a suburban shopping center and then makes a short loop through the countryside just west of Lexington. Despite its modest length, it takes in a variety of rural landscapes. You pass fields containing all the region's main agricultural products: horses, cattle, tobacco, and corn. You also see examples of the most recent and most lucrative Bluegrass crop: the 3,000-square-foot, brick-veneer mini-mansion sitting on its own acre lot.

Criticizing such houses is easy, but I try to keep my self-righteousness in check. Every house probably offended someone when it was built. There is a long Bluegrass tradition of building the fanciest house one can afford, and over the years that tradition has produced some real beauties.

The route takes in two counties that have different attitudes toward suburban development, and you can see the difference as you ride. Fayette County, which includes the city of Lexington, has strict land-use laws. The county is divided into an urban zone, where dense development is encouraged, and a much bigger rural zone, where (except in some existing villages) a new house must have at least 25 acres of land around it. The line between urban and rural is sharp. You can see it clearly near the end of this ride, just past mile 15. You pedal through a completely rural scene, and

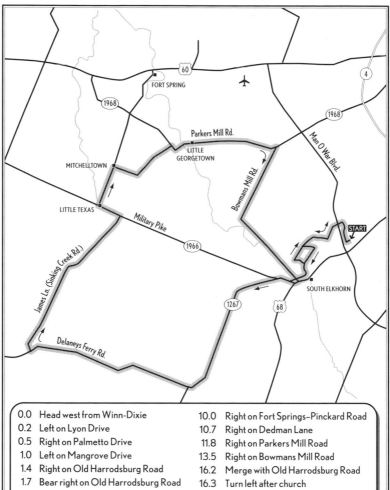

0.0	Head west from Winn-Dixie
0.2	Left on Lyon Drive
0.5	Right on Palmetto Drive
1.0	Left on Mangrove Drive
1.4	Right on Old Harrodsburg Road
1.7	Bear right on Old Harrodsburg Road
1.8	Right on Military Pike (KY 1267)
2.0	Left at the fork
4.4	Straight on Delaneys Ferry Road
7.0	Right on James Lane
9.7	Left on Military Pike (KY 1966)
10.0	Right on Fort Springs–Pinckard Road
10.7	Right on Dedman Lane
11.8	Right on Parkers Mill Road
13.5	Right on Bowmans Mill Road
16.2	Merge with Old Harrodsburg Road
16.3	Turn left after church
16.5	Left on Madrone Way
16.7	Right on Palmetto Drive
17.3	Left on Lyon Drive
17.5	Right after the Shell station
17.8	End at Winn-Dixie

4. LEXINGTON WEST

then all at once you see the side-by-side houses of the urban zone looming like the wall of a medieval town.

Jessamine County, in contrast, allows suburban development on 1-acre lots. That is where you'll find the mini-mansions.

DIRECTIONS FOR THE RIDE

The ride begins at the Palomar Shopping Center in Lexington, where Harrodsburg Road crosses Man O War Boulevard. You can reach the start by Lexington city bus. Take the Number 5 south to the end of the line.

0.0 Start at the Winn-Dixie parking lot and head west (toward McDonald's).

0.2 Left on Lyon Drive. Go straight through the traffic light into the Palomar Hills subdivision.

0.5 Right on Palmetto Drive.

1.0 Left on Mangrove Drive. At mile 1.2 Mangrove makes a sharp bend right.

1.4 Cross Madrone Way and enter a church driveway. If the gate is closed, look left for the opening in the fence. Follow the driveway around to the left of the church buildings. Pass the church entrance, with its two red doors, and turn right on Old Harrodsburg Road.

1.7 Stay on Old Harrodsburg Road as Bowmans Mill Road forks off to the right.
The street signs are misleading. Just keep left and you'll be fine. The road now crosses South Elkhorn Creek on a bridge with twin stone arches.

1.8 Right on Military Pike (KY 1267).

2.0 Left (almost straight, actually) at the fork. The route number remains KY 1267, but starting here it's called Keene–Troy Road.

3.0 Enter Jessamine County.

4.4 Straight as Keene–Troy Road turns left. Without turning, you are now on Delaneys Ferry Road.

7.0 Right on James Lane. Old maps show this as Sinking Creek Road.

7.9 Pass a striking example of a sink on the right.

Sinks are bowl-like geologic features from which water sinks into underground channels instead of flowing away into a surface stream. Sinks are common in the Bluegrass, but this one is bigger and more distinct than most.

9.7   Left on Military Pike at a T-junction.

10.0   Right on Fort Springs–Pinckard Road.

10.7   Right on Dedman Lane.
This is classic horse-farm country. Big trees line both sides of the road, with neat bluegrass fields bordered by traditional plank fences just beyond.

11.8   Right on Parkers Mill Road.

12.4   Enter Little Georgetown, a row of modest houses with long back gardens that slope down to Elkhorn Creek.
The population is mainly, if not wholly, African American. Before the abolition of slavery, most blacks lived on their owners' farms. Once free, they continued to work on the big farms but needed new places to live, so they settled in all-black

The bridge over South Elkhorn Creek.

villages. Many of their descendants still live in these villages, though today they are more likely to work in Lexington.

12.8 Cross Airport Road.
A short side trip up this road takes you to the Aviation Museum.

13.5 Right on Bowmans Mill Road.
A couple of steep hills lie ahead. At mile 14.5 the road passes a tower shaped like the turret of a castle.

15.8 Pass the Cedar Hall–Helm Place.
This columned mansion was built before the Civil War. Alas, it's not open to the public.

16.2 Merge with Old Harrodsburg Road as Bowmans Mill Road swings left on its approach to the village of South Elkhorn.

16.3 Pass South Elkhorn Church and turn left. Aim for the black fence with suburban houses behind it.

16.5 Left on Madrone Way as you leave the church property.

16.7 Right on Palmetto Drive.

17.3 Left on Lyon Drive.

17.5 Cross Man O War Boulevard, a four-lane divided highway, and turn right behind the Shell station.

17.8 End at the Winn-Dixie parking lot.

Bicycle Shops

Dodds Cyclery, 1985 Harrodsburg Road, Lexington; 859-277-6013

Pedal Power, 401 South Upper Street, Lexington; 859-255-6408

Scheller's, 212 Woodland Avenue, Lexington; 859-233-1764

Vicious Cycle, Todds Road at Codell, Lexington; 859-263-7300

5

Whiskey Rivers

- **DISTANCE:** 18.1 miles (21.2 miles including alternate route)
- **HIGHLIGHTS:** Two bourbon distilleries, Young's High Bridge, and the chance to ford the Salt River

Though this tour stays within one county, it explores two of Kentucky's great rivers. The Kentucky and Salt Rivers come within 4 miles of each other, but could hardly differ more. The Kentucky is a wide, navigable waterway that flows through a deep gorge on its way north to join the Ohio River at Carrollton. The Salt is a much smaller stream. It flows through a broad, gentle valley, heading west to join the Ohio near Louisville.

Each river has a bourbon distillery. The Kentucky River's distillery is at Tyrone and makes Wild Turkey. The Salt River's distillery is at Bond's Mill and makes Four Roses. Both offer public tours.

Bourbon whiskey originated in the Bluegrass and was named for Bourbon County, which is northeast of Lexington. Shipped all over the world, most of it is still produced in Kentucky (not, however, in Bourbon County, which no longer has any distilleries).

Bourbon's distinctive taste comes from corn—which, by law, must make up over half the mash—and from aging in charred oak barrels. When it first comes out of the still, bourbon is as clear as water. It gets its color from its long stay in those charred barrels. Old-timers sometimes called it red liquor, to distinguish it from the raw white stuff sold without government tax stamps. Some folks in

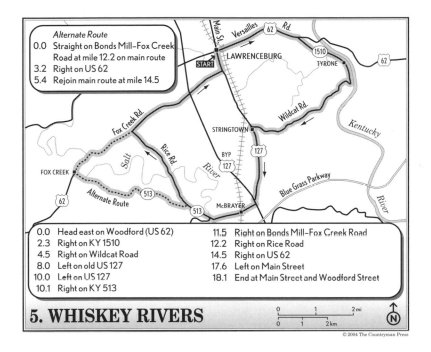

Alternate Route

0.0	Straight on Bonds Mill–Fox Creek Road at mile 12.2 on main route
3.2	Right on US 62
5.4	Rejoin main route at mile 14.5

0.0	Head east on Woodford (US 62)
2.3	Right on KY 1510
4.5	Right on Wildcat Road
8.0	Left on old US 127
10.0	Left on US 127
10.1	Right on KY 513

11.5	Right on Bonds Mill–Fox Creek Road
12.2	Right on Rice Road
14.5	Right on US 62
17.6	Left on Main Street
18.1	End at Main Street and Woodford Street

5. WHISKEY RIVERS

© 2004 The Countryman Press

the Bluegrass may still make white liquor, but their stills don't show up on maps.

Stripped of its romance, a bourbon distillery is really just a chemical-processing plant. That fact became clear a few years back when a fire broke out in one of Tyrone's whiskey warehouses. A huge volume of flaming bourbon coursed down a creek, torching all the trees in its path. The fire sizzled out as the spill reached the Kentucky River, but alcohol killed fish for miles downstream. Now, that's a whiskey river.

This tour includes three challenging roads, and each tests the rider in a different way. The first is US 62, a shoulderless road that carries substantial traffic, including heavy trucks. There is no practical way to avoid it. The second is Wildcat Road, which serves up a mile-long climb without benefit of pavement. It's not bad as dirt roads go, but expect it to be a little sloppy and slippery in wet weather. The third challenge comes on Rice Road, which crosses the Salt River at a ford. Plan to get your feet wet. If the water is too high to ford, an alternate route takes you to a bridge.

DIRECTIONS FOR THE RIDE

Start at the corner of Main Street and Woodford Street in downtown Lawrenceburg. You should have no trouble parking your car nearby.

0.0 Head east on Woodford Street (US 62).

0.1 Cross railroad tracks.

0.6 Pass a small shopping center with two convenience stores.

2.3 Right on KY 1510.
Boxy warehouses for aging bourbon whiskey line the road. Just ahead is the Wild Turkey distillery.

2.9 Pass the remains of a dismantled railroad overpass.
Trains used to cross here to and from Young's High Bridge.

3.1 Stop partway down the hill.
Pull off the road to look back at two big bridges spanning the Kentucky River Gorge. The shorter is the Blackburn Memorial Bridge, which carries US 62 road traffic. The longer is Young's High Bridge, with a main span of 551 feet. It carried trains from 1889 to 1985, but now faces an uncertain future. One group hopes to preserve it as a scenic railroad. Another group wants to make it part of a rail-trail, which would open it to bicycles. No one seems to want it torn down, but that is what will happen unless the preservationists figure out how to pay for its maintenance.

3.6 Cross a small bridge and enter Tyrone.
Tyrone has seen better days. It was once an incorporated town with over 900 residents. But that was before Prohibition, which was tough on towns that made bourbon for a living. The distillery came back to life when liquor became legal again, but the town never recovered. Today it's an unincorporated village.

4.5 Right on Wildcat Road, a twisting, one-lane dirt road.
What it lacks in pavement, it makes up for in scenery. The steep land is heavily treed, and on the left Wildcat Creek flows down a steep ravine. In the Bluegrass, the name "Wildcat" almost always honors the University of Kentucky's basketball

Wildcat Road near Tyrone.

team. But this creek and road are so remote that the presence of real wildcats—the four-footed kind—seems plausible.

5.5 Pavement resumes, but it's not much smoother than the dirt.
The road remains narrow, and gets even steeper till you reach the Bluegrass Plateau at mile 10.5.

8.0 Left on old US 127.
This is Stringtown. Kentucky has several Stringtowns, and all are accurately named. They stretch out like strings along a single road. If you were to go straight here, in half a mile you would reach the site of the Salt River Baptist Church, founded in 1798. The first minister here was John Penney. His grandson, who went by the initials "J. C.," founded a department store you may have heard of.

10.0 Left on US 127, a four-lane divided highway with paved shoulders.

10.1 Right on KY 513.

If you need to stop at a store, stay on US 127 for a few yards past this turn and you'll find one at the Blue Grass Parkway interchange.

10.6 Cross railroad tracks and enter the village of McBrayer.
Beyond McBrayer (no services) the road starts a long, gentle descent to the Salt River. The Salt River Valley spreads out before you on both sides.

11.4 Pass the Four Roses distillery.

11.5 Cross the Salt River.
Note the old bridge piers to the right of the modern bridge. They supported a covered bridge for over a century.

The Salt is one of Kentucky's great rivers, though it hardly looks like one this far upstream. In state politics, the phrase "up Salt River" means "defeated." This phrase has its origins in the presidential campaign of 1832, in which local boy Henry Clay went up against Andrew Jackson. Clay boarded a steamboat in Bullitt County, planning to go down to Louisville for a speech. Someone from the other side bribed the steamboat's master to head upstream instead, causing Clay to miss his appointment.

11.5 Right on Bonds Mill–Fox Creek Road.
At mile 12.0 look right for a tiny cemetery completely enclosed by stone walls. To get in, you have to leap over the wall. Graves here date from the 1860s.

12.2 Right on Rice Road.
This is a one-lane road with rough pavement. Watch for loose gravel.

13.1 Ford the Salt River.
But don't do it unless you are sure the water is low enough for a safe crossing. People drown in places like this. If you have the slightest doubt about your ability to cross, turn around and take the alternate route described at the end of this chapter. You can always come back another day to try the ford.

Fords used to be common all over the Bluegrass, but few remain these days. Some became unusable when dams raised water levels, but most were replaced by bridges and live on only in the names of roads and towns. Frankfort, the state capital, started out as Frank's Ford. But you can't ford the river there anymore.

14.5 Right on US 62.

15.1 Pass a country store.

16.4 Cross US 127 Bypass.
You'll find an assortment of franchise restaurants here. For local flavor, ride on to the Broadway Diner at mile 17.

17.6 Left on Main Street, which leads to downtown Lawrenceburg and several eating places.
In keeping with the bourbon-making tradition, Lawrenceburg is Kentucky's only county seat named for a tavern owner.

18.1 End the ride at the corner of Main Street and Woodford Street.

Alternate Route

Go this way if you don't want to ford the Salt River. Mileage starts at the intersection of Bonds Mill–Fox Creek Road and Rice Road, which is mile 12.2 on the main route.

0.0 Straight on Bonds Mill–Fox Creek Road.
Wouldn't you just hate to have to write out that address all the time? The rock fences on this road differ from what you normally see in the Bluegrass. The usual design leaves most of the rocks lying flat, with one layer of slanted rocks on top. But in the Anderson County design all the rocks are slanted.

3.2 Right on US 62 at a T-junction.
For a quarter mile or so before reaching this junction you can see the Salt River on the right, far below the road.

4.0 Cross the Salt River.

5.4 Pass the north end of Rice Lane.
This is where you would have come out if you had taken the ford. You pick up the main route again at mile 14.5.

Bicycle Shops

If you need repairs or parts, head to Lexington or Danville.

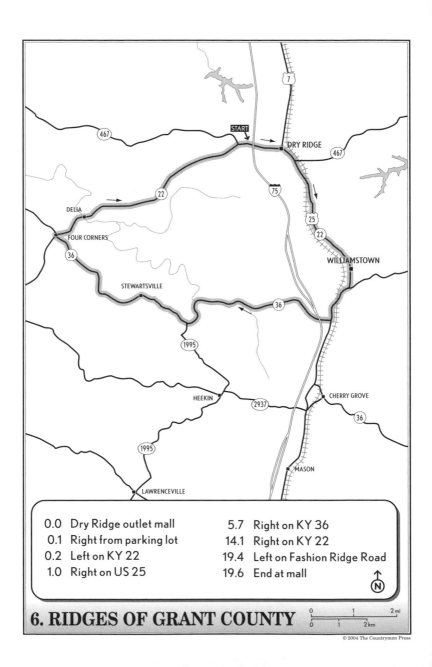

0.0	Dry Ridge outlet mall	5.7	Right on KY 36
0.1	Right from parking lot	14.1	Right on KY 22
0.2	Left on KY 22	19.4	Left on Fashion Ridge Road
1.0	Right on US 25	19.6	End at mall

6. RIDGES OF GRANT COUNTY

© 2004 The Countryman Press

Ridges of Grant County

- **DISTANCE:** 19.6 miles
- **HIGHLIGHTS:** Downtown Williamstown, ridgetop views, and a short ride on the Dixie Highway

This tour, starting as it does at a nondescript freeway exit, points up the huge difference between modern car travel and bicycle touring. Thousands of cars and trucks pass through Grant County on I-75. It's the primary road between Cincinnati and Lexington, and it serves as a main route for midwesterners and Canadians driving to Florida. Those motorists barely see the county. Most don't stop at all. And of the few who do, almost no one ventures beyond the gas stations, motels, and stores that cluster around the interstate exits.

That's a shame, because Grant County is worth a look. And on your bike it's easy to leave the freeway and see what the country-side has to offer.

This tour begins at a freeway outlet mall, makes its way through the small towns of Dry Ridge and Williamstown, and then heads out into the thinly populated countryside. You are riding in the Eden Shale Belt, also called the Hills of the Bluegrass. It's hilly all right, and yet much of the ride is on level roadway. One word explains the level riding—ridges.

Roads in the Eden Shale Belt typically follow ridges. The land goes up and down, but the road doesn't—as long as it stays atop that ridge. Some roads follow creeks instead of ridges, but that's

Grant County Courthouse in Williamstown.

okay because the creek valleys are level, too. Problems arise only where the road drops off one ridgetop and ascends another. At such places you can expect a wild downhill ride, followed by a tough climb. Still, rides in this part of the Bluegrass usually involve only a few steep grades, with lots of level ridgetop roadway in between.

Thanks to ridgetop roads, the Eden Shale Belt often provides easier riding than the so-called rolling plain of the Inner Bluegrass, where roads march straight across the landscape, veering only where they encounter something really big like the Kentucky River Gorge. The hills may be small, but the roads hit them all. Thus, the roads of the Inner Bluegrass tend to be straight but sloped. That approach to road building would never work in a place like Grant County, because the hills are too steep. Roads here are curvy but level for the most part. And when you're on a bike, curvy and level beats straight and sloped every time.

DIRECTIONS FOR THE RIDE

0.0 Start at the Dry Ridge outlet mall at Exit 159 on I-75.
This exit is roughly midway between Cincinnati and Lexington.

0.1 Right on leaving the mall parking lot.

0.2 Left on KY 22, crossing over I-75.
You can find the usual assortment of fast-food restaurants and motels here. Behind you on KY 22 there is a decent local place, the Country Grill, but don't turn around yet. You'll get there near the end of the ride, when you'll be much hungrier.

1.0 Right on US 25, in the center of Dry Ridge.
For the next 4.7 miles the route follows the Dixie Highway, though no signs say so. Before the interstates and numbered U.S. highways, roads with real names crisscrossed America. Some of the names still evoke romance and adventure: the Lincoln Highway running from coast to coast, the Old Spanish Trail in the Southwest, the Meridian Highway cutting through the country's empty center. The Dixie Highway went from northern Michigan to southern Florida, passing through Kentucky along the way.

The Dixie Highway gave birth to Kentucky's best-known business: Kentucky Fried Chicken, started by Colonel Sanders. The highway made Sanders's fortune twice: first by bringing traffic his way, and then by taking it away when the inter-state came through. It's not really a Bluegrass story since it happened in Corbin. But it's still a good story.

After working a variety of jobs, Harland Sanders moved to Corbin in 1930 and opened a gas station. The business prospered, thanks to tourists on the Dixie Highway. He added a restaurant and motel, and by 1937 Sanders' Cafe had 142 seats. The most popular dish was fried chicken, made to Sanders's special recipe.

So far, so good. But we wouldn't know Sanders's name today if he had contin-ued running a modestly successful diner, even if his chicken tasted pretty good. His "break" came when I-75 arrived in Corbin and stole all the long-distance travelers from the Dixie Highway. Knowing he couldn't survive much longer in Corbin, Sanders sold his place and took his show on the road. He first sold franchises for his Kentucky Fried Chicken in Salt Lake City, and eventually around the world.

1.9 Cross sharply angled railroad tracks.
Take care not to fall.

2.5 Enter Williamstown, the Grant County seat.

4.8 Angle slightly right as you pass the courthouse in downtown Williamstown.
You can eat at Alice's Restaurant in town. Contrary to the Arlo Guthrie song (which was set in New England, anyway), you cannot get anything you want here. But if your wants are limited to a sandwich and coffee, they can fix you up.

5.3 Cross over railroad tracks.
Watch out, as the tracks cross the road at a sharp angle.

5.7 Right on KY 36.
There is a convenience store on the corner.

6.0 Cross over I-75.
This freeway interchange has two motels and two restaurants. Surprisingly, neither restaurant is part of a national chain. It's all countryside for the rest of the ride. Grant County has its share of working farms, but much of the land is reverting to nature. Instead of crops you find cedars and wild turkeys.

9.2 Cross Clarks Creek after a descent from the ridgetop.
Just before the bridge a rough dirt road leads to the creek bank, in case you want a closer look.

11.1 Enter Stewartsville (no services).
The hillsides are steep here, but the road continues to wind along the ridgetop.

14.1 Right on KY 22.

15.0 Cross Clarks Creek again.

19.2 Enter the outskirts of Dry Ridge.
There's a supermarket on the left, and the Country Grill is on the right. The name might sound like a franchise, but this is a good, locally owned restaurant. Folks were stopping here to eat long before the outlet mall went up.

19.4 Left on Fashion Ridge Road, just beyond the Speedway store.

19.6 End at the outlet mall parking lot.

Bicycle Shops

I hope you don't need one, because if you do it will mean a trip to Lexington or the Cincinnati suburbs.

Lodging

A Hampton Inn (859-823-7111) and Holiday Inn Express (859-824-7121) are located right at the outlet mall, and across the interstate you'll find a Microtel (859-824-2000), Super 8 (859-824-3700), and the Dry Ridge Motor Inn (859-824-7005). All of these are at Exit 159 on I-75. Two more motels, a Days Inn (859-824-5025) and a Best Value Inn (859-824-7177), are beside Exit 154. This exit is at mile 6.0 on the route, and you could easily start there.

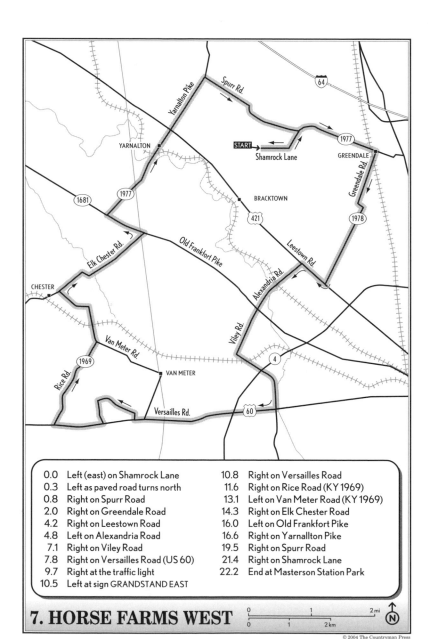

0.0	Left (east) on Shamrock Lane	10.8	Right on Versailles Road
0.3	Left as paved road turns north	11.6	Right on Rice Road (KY 1969)
0.8	Right on Spurr Road	13.1	Left on Van Meter Road (KY 1969)
2.0	Right on Greendale Road	14.3	Right on Elk Chester Road
4.2	Right on Leestown Road	16.0	Left on Old Frankfort Pike
4.8	Left on Alexandria Road	16.6	Right on Yarnallton Pike
7.1	Right on Viley Road	19.5	Right on Spurr Road
7.8	Right on Versailles Road (US 60)	21.4	Right on Shamrock Lane
9.7	Right at the traffic light	22.2	End at Masterson Station Park
10.5	Left at sign GRANDSTAND EAST		

7. HORSE FARMS WEST

Horse Farms West

- **DISTANCE:** 22.2 miles
- **HIGHLIGHTS:** Rock fences, Keeneland Race Course, and some of the world's most famous and scenic horse farms

People raise horses all over the Bluegrass. Horse farms are not all alike, however. The farms that made the Bluegrass famous—the farms where racing thoroughbreds are bred and trained—lie in a band that wraps around the north side of Lexington. This tour takes you through the west part of that area.

It begins at a former horse farm that is now a city park catering to horse people and passes more than a dozen working horse farms, including the famous Calumet, before running through the grounds of the Keeneland Race Course.

Pay attention to the fences. They say a lot about the farms they enclose. The fanciest horse farms all have plank fences, with four, or sometimes three, horizontal planks. Not long ago such fences were always white; now many are black. Apparently, no other colors are allowed. The more modest horse farms have a different style of fence, with a single plank on top and wire mesh underneath.

Dirt farms, which raise ordinary crops like corn and tobacco instead of horses, have plain wire fences like farms anywhere. Mixed in with all those working fences is a much older type: the dry-laid stone wall, which Kentuckians call a rock fence. It's made of local limestone laid without mortar, and some examples go back to the mid-1800s. The number of rock fences fell drastically in the 20th century, but the tide may have turned. People are now repairing the old walls and even laying new ones.

Part of this tour follows the "Horse Farm Tour 2" in the *WPA Guide to Kentucky,* published in 1939. Surprisingly little has changed since then. I guess when you have something as good as a Kentucky horse farm, you don't mess with it.

Services are scarce on this route, despite its proximity to Lexington. The only place to buy food is at Keeneland, and even there breakfast is the only meal you can count on year-round.

DIRECTIONS FOR THE RIDE

The tour starts at Masterson Station Park, located on Leestown Road in Lexington's western outskirts. If you arrive by car, drive past all the soccer fields and park near the intersection of Shamrock Lane and Ruffian Way. You can also reach the tour by Lexington city bus. Take the Number 6 (Leestown Road) bus and get off at the Coca-Cola plant. You'll start the tour at mile 4.1.

0.0 Left (east) on Shamrock Lane as you leave the Masterson Station parking lot.
The word "station" appears in many Bluegrass place-names, and it has a special meaning that dates to the 1700s. A station was a group of buildings set up for protection against Indian attack. Stations resembled forts, but were smaller and did not serve the general public.

This city park is rare in that horses are not only allowed but welcomed. Riders who aren't wealthy enough to own horse farms come here to train and exercise their steeds.

0.3 Left as the paved road turns sharply north at the intersection with a gravel lane.
A picnic area with drinking water is straight ahead.

0.8 Right on Spurr Road, where Shamrock Lane ends at a T-junction.

1.8 Cross the Norfolk Southern railroad tracks.

2.0 Right on Greendale Road.

4.1 Pass the Coca-Cola bottling plant.

Alas, they don't offer free samples. You can also reach this spot by Lexington city bus.

4.2 Right on Leestown Road.
Traffic can be heavy here, but you have to deal with it for less than a mile.

4.8 Left on Alexandria Road. (Some maps still show this as Viley Road.)
If you have been less than impressed by the scenery for the last couple of miles, take heart. It soon gets a lot better.

5.3 Cross railroad tracks and Town Branch Creek.
This railroad is the oldest in the state.

6.7 Pass Calumet Farm on your right.
You'll get a better view later.

6.8 Slow down for railroad tracks.
They are rough and cross the road diagonally.

The famous Keeneland Race Course attracts cyclists as well as horserace fans.

7.1 Right on Viley Road.

7.8 Right on Versailles Road (US 60).
This is a very busy road, but thanks to wide lanes and paved shoulders it's not bad for cycling. If you crave food or drink, turn left instead and in half a mile you'll reach a commercial district packed with restaurants and stores.

8.1 Cross New Circle Road (KY 4).
Calumet Farm is on your right, behind a fancy red gate and long white fences. This is probably the best-known horse farm in the world. It was named for the Calumets, who made their fortune selling baking powder. In the 1930s very few American houses had air-conditioning, but Calumet's stallion barn did. Remember the villain's Kentucky horse farm in the James Bond movie Goldfinger? *That was Calumet.*

9.7 Right at the traffic light at the Keeneland entrance, opposite Man O War Boulevard.
The farm at the southeast corner trades in exotic livestock. Instead of racehorses you might see alpacas or longhorn cattle munching the bluegrass.

10.5 Left at the track where you see the sign GRANDSTAND EAST.
Keeneland is more than a racetrack. To locals, it's almost a city park. Joggers love it, and the Bluegrass Cycling Club starts many rides here. To horse people, it's a holy shrine. Keeneland is to horseracing what Wimbledon is to tennis or St. Andrew's to golf. Many city racetracks are located in rough neighborhoods and have a gritty look, but Keeneland sits in splendor amid trees and fields.

If you time it right, you can eat breakfast at the Track Kitchen in the barn area north of the track. It's open most mornings, even when no races are scheduled. The food is good, but the people are the main attraction. Everybody in the horse business eats here, from millionaire owners to stable hands.

10.8 Right on Versailles Road.

11.6 Right on Rice Road (KY 1969).
A short but steep grade lies just ahead. From the top of the hill you can see the front of the Keeneland grandstand.

13.1 Left on Van Meter Road (still KY 1969).

14.3 Right on Elk Chester Road.
There are a few scruffy dirt farms nearby, proving that not every Bluegrass farm has fast horses and a rich owner. Watch for chickens in the road.

16.0 Left on Old Frankfort Pike.
Many Bluegrass roads are called pikes. They used to be toll roads—turnpikes—where you had to pay a fee before the guard turned the pike and let you pass. The tolls disappeared many years ago, but the name stuck around. Little by little the pikes are disappearing, though. Lexington old-timers call almost every road a pike, but modern usage has converted many of them into just plain roads.

16.6 Right on Yarnallton Pike.
Horse country doesn't get any better than this: white fences on one side, black on the other, with green grass and fancy barns as far as the eye can see.

18.0 Cross railroad tracks.

18.4 Cross Leestown Road.
The horse farm on the northwest corner is unusual in that it's almost treeless.

18.8 Pass an interesting rock fence on the right.
It's said to be in the Scottish style, as opposed to the usual Irish.

19.5 Right on Spurr Road.

20.3 Follow Spurr Road as it bends right.
That's no horse farm straight ahead. It's a federal penitentiary.

21.4 Right on Shamrock Lane.

22.2 End the ride at Masterson Station Park.

Bicycle Shops

Dodds Cyclery, 1985 Harrodsburg Road, Lexington; 859-277-6013

Pedal Power, 401 South Upper Street, Lexington; 859-255-6408

Scheller's, 212 Woodland Avenue, Lexington; 859-233-1764

Vicious Cycle, Todds Road at Codell, Lexington; 859-263-7300

Lodging

The city of Lexington has a wide range of hotels and motels. Camping is available at the Lexington Horse Park, just off the route to the northeast. It makes a good base if you plan to ride both horse-farm tours.

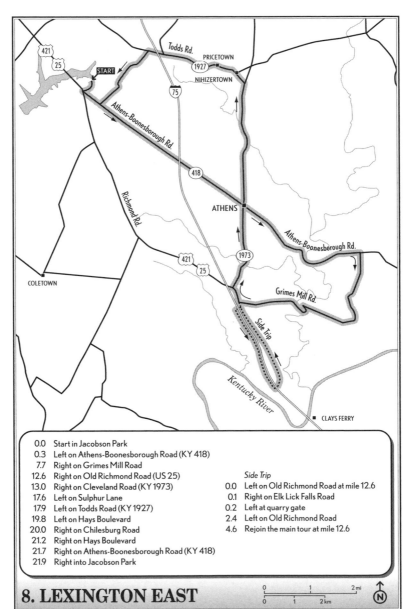

0.0	Start in Jacobson Park
0.3	Left on Athens-Boonesborough Road (KY 418)
7.7	Right on Grimes Mill Road
12.6	Right on Old Richmond Road (US 25)
13.0	Right on Cleveland Road (KY 1973)
17.6	Left on Sulphur Lane
17.9	Left on Todds Road (KY 1927)
19.8	Left on Hays Boulevard
20.0	Right on Chilesburg Road
21.2	Right on Hays Boulevard
21.7	Right on Athens-Boonesborough Road (KY 418)
21.9	Right into Jacobson Park

Side Trip

0.0	Left on Old Richmond Road at mile 12.6
0.1	Right on Elk Lick Falls Road
0.2	Left at quarry gate
2.4	Left on Old Richmond Road
4.6	Rejoin the main tour at mile 12.6

8. LEXINGTON EAST

© 2004 The Countryman Press

Lexington East

- **DISTANCE:** 22.3 miles (26.9 miles including alternate route.)
- **HIGHLIGHTS:** The hunt country, Boone Creek, and one of the steepest paved roads in the Bluegrass

Like Ride 4: Lexington West, this tour starts in the suburbs but quickly reaches the countryside. This is not wilderness, however. It's settled country; people have lived and farmed here for over 200 years. The earliest settlers included Daniel Boone, who founded Boone Station (now a state historic site) about a mile east of present-day Athens. He moved here because Fort Boonesborough had grown too crowded to suit him. You have to wonder what he would think of modern Lexington or Louisville.

If you ride here from November to April, don't be surprised to encounter hunters on horseback wearing red coats and blue vests and accompanied by hounds. They still call it foxhunting, though the quarry these days is more likely to be a coyote. Oscar Wilde once said "the English country gentleman galloping after a fox is the unspeakable in full pursuit of the uneatable," but that doesn't seem fair in Kentucky. The hunters seem like decent chaps. I have yet to meet the coyotes.

You can reach this ride by Lexington city bus. Ride the Number 6 bus out Richmond Road, getting off where the bus turns left at Eagle Creek Drive. On your bike, continue on Richmond Road across the reservoir. In 1.3 miles you will reach the entrance to Jacobson Park, which is mile 0.3 on the tour.

DIRECTIONS FOR THE RIDE

Start in Jacobson Park, near the marina. The park is located in Lexington's southwest suburbs, on Richmond Road about 2 miles beyond Man O War Boulevard. If you are driving in from I-75, take Exit 104. Head toward Lexington on KY 418 and look for the park on your right.

0.0 Ride to the park entrance.

0.3 Left on Athens–Boonesborough Road (KY 418) on leaving Jacobson Park.
This four-lane divided highway gets heavy traffic but is easy to ride thanks to a wide shoulder and little cross traffic.

2.9 Cross I-75.
Five national motel chains have set up shop here, along with a few restaurants and convenience stores. KY 418 continues, but almost all the cars and trucks peel off at the interstate.

4.5 Cross Cleveland Road (KY 1973) in the heart of Athens.
This village used to be called Cross Plains for the two buffalo traces that crossed here. You'll find a small grocery store in town.

Turn left if you want to visit Boone Station State Historic Site. It's about a mile off the route. Daniel and his family founded Boone Station in 1779, but he moved on after a few years. He never stayed anywhere for long.

6.0 Cross McCall Mill Road and start a steep descent.

6.5 Cross Boone Creek.
After heavy rains, the creek becomes one of the best whitewater streams in Kentucky. It only happens once or twice a year, but when it does the kayakers come running. Don't try it unless you are well skilled, though. A few years back a very experienced kayaker drowned here.

After the creek comes a climb, which will probably slow you down enough that you can get a good look at the rock fence on your left. It's a beauty.

7.7 Right on Grimes Mill Road.

9.2 Pass St. Hubert's Church.
It's just a small country church, but it draws a crowd every November when the bishop comes out from Lexington for the Blessing of the Hounds. If you have a few

St. Hubert Church in foxhunting country.

minutes to spare, wander around to the back of the church where a grassy lane leads to a garden and small cemetery.

Less than a mile beyond the church, the road starts a very steep descent to Boone Creek's mini-gorge. It's fun to go fast down a steep road, but don't forget that there is a hairpin curve near the bottom.

10.8 Cross Boone Creek on an old steel bridge.
This has to be one of the loveliest spots in the Bluegrass. The creek flows over a rocky bed at the bottom of a narrow gorge. It remains cool and shady down here on the hottest summer days. Just over the bridge is the big stone building that houses the Iroquois Hunt Club. It used to be a mill.

And now it's time to gear down, screw up your courage—or whatever it is you do when a really hard climb looms. The road out of the gorge is the steepest stretch of pavement you'll find on any tour in this book. I won't say it's the steepest paved road in the entire Bluegrass, because when you say things like that someone always comes along to prove you wrong. But it's steep.

Don't forget to check the view to your right as you climb. You can see the gorge, the bridge, and the road you just took, all far below you now.

12.6 Right on Old Richmond Road (US 25) at the T-junction.
If you're up to it, a side trip here offers a view of the Kentucky River Gorge (see below).

13.0 Right on Cleveland Road (KY 1973).

14.9 Cross Athens–Boonesborough Road in the center of Athens. (You should recognize this crossroads; you were here back at mile 4.5.) Stay on Cleveland Road.
Two short blocks ahead, Gentry Road heads off to the right. Turn here if you want to visit Boone Station State Historic Site but didn't do so earlier in the ride.

17.6 Left on Sulphur Lane.

17.9 Left on Todds Road (KY 1927).

19.7 Cross over I-75.
You are now getting back into the Lexington suburbs.

19.8 Left on Hays Boulevard.
The directions from here to mile 21.2 are accurate at the time of this writing. But the area is being developed for houses, and the road layout may soon change.

Eventually, you will be able to stay on Hays Boulevard all the way from Todds Road to Athens-Boonesborough Road.

20.0 Right on Chilesburg Road.

21.2 Right on Hays Boulevard.

21.7 Right on Athens-Boonesborough Road (KY 418).

21.9 Right into Jacobson Park.

22.3 End your ride at the parking lot near the marina.

Side Trip

This side trip offers views of the Kentucky River Gorge. It starts at mile 12.6 on the main tour and adds 4.6 miles to the ride.

0.0 Start at the intersection of Grimes Mill and Old Richmond Roads (mile 12.6 on the main tour). Turn left from Grimes Mill Road.

0.1 Right on Elk Lick Falls Road and pass through a short tunnel under I-75.

0.2 Left at quarry gate.
In about 2 miles the landscape on the right opens up and you can see the Kentucky River Gorge.

2.4 Left on Old Richmond Road, which takes you over I-75.
You get another good view of the gorge near mile 2.8.

3.5 Pass a country store.

4.6 Cross Grimes Mill Road.
Stay on Old Richmond Road to resume the main tour where you jumped off at mile 12.6.

Bicycle Shops

Dodds Cyclery, 1985 Harrodsburg Road, Lexington; 859-277-6013

Pedal Power, 401 South Upper Street, Lexington; 859-255-6408

Scheller's, 212 Woodland Avenue, Lexington; 859-233-1764

Vicious Cycle, Todds Road at Codell, Lexington; 859-263-7300

Lodging

Choose from five modern motels: Comfort Suites (859-263-0777), Days Inn (859-263-3100), Econolodge (859-263-5101), Holiday Inn (859-263-5241), and Red Roof Inn (859-543-1877). All are at Exit 104 on I-75, or mile 2.9 on the bike tour. If you prefer camping, head to Fort Boonesborough State Park.

9

The Asparagus Patch

- **DISTANCE:** 22.7 miles
- **HIGHLIGHTS:** Horse farms, an old distillery, and a thrilling descent into the Kentucky River Gorge

If the Bluegrass is a garden—goes the old saying—Woodford County is its asparagus patch. The fertility of the Inner Bluegrass is nowhere more evident than right here. Woodford ranks near the top of Kentucky counties in farm income, with products ranging from field corn to wine grapes. It stands second only to next-door-neighbor Fayette County in the fame of its thoroughbred horse farms.

You could spend days wandering the county roads at random without running out of good scenery and good cycling routes. You should try it sometime. But if you don't have much time to explore, this tour packs a lot of Woodford County into less than 23 miles.

DIRECTIONS FOR THE RIDE

Start in downtown Versailles, at the public parking lot off Rose Hill Street. To get to the lot, first find the courthouse. Go south on Main Street, turn right at the light, and then right again into the lot.

0.0 Right on Rose Hill Street as you leave the parking lot.

0.3 Keep straight on KY 1964 as US 62, along with most of the traffic, forks left.

0.6 Pass a small grocery store.

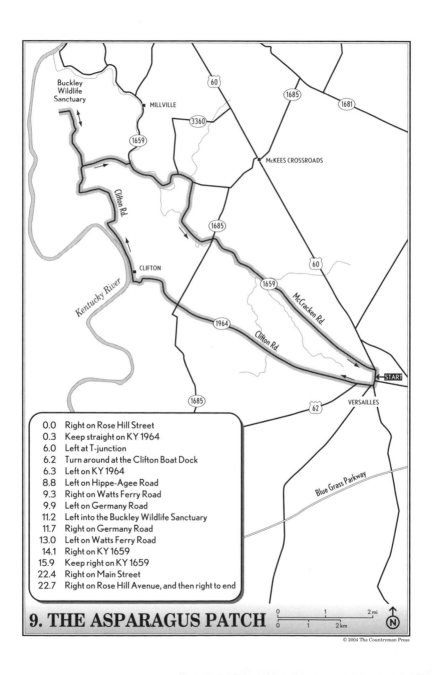

0.0	Right on Rose Hill Street
0.3	Keep straight on KY 1964
6.0	Left at T-junction
6.2	Turn around at the Clifton Boat Dock
6.3	Left on KY 1964
8.8	Left on Hippe-Agee Road
9.3	Right on Watts Ferry Road
9.9	Left on Germany Road
11.2	Left into the Buckley Wildlife Sanctuary
11.7	Right on Germany Road
13.0	Left on Watts Ferry Road
14.1	Right on KY 1659
15.9	Keep right on KY 1659
22.4	Right on Main Street
22.7	Right on Rose Hill Avenue, and then right to end

9. THE ASPARAGUS PATCH

0.7 Cross railroad tracks.
The crossing is rough and diagonal.

5.2 Start your descent into the Kentucky River Gorge.
For the next mile the road twists its way down to river level. Limestone cliffs line the left side of the road. On the right, a creek flows through a steep ravine. Watch your speed, because a T-junction awaits at the bottom of the hill.

6.0 Left at the T-junction.
The Kentucky River lies straight ahead.

6.2 Turn around at the Clifton Boat Dock.
This dock was a base for commercial fishing as recently as the 1980s. The business is now closed, but it provides a good spot from which to view the river. A pole stuck in the riverbank measures the water level during floods, which can make a mess of Clifton.

6.3 Left on KY 1964.
Clifton village occupies the thin strip of land between road and river. A ferry ran here for many years. It capsized in 1925. Six sheep and a cow drowned, but a Louisville newspaper reported that "several men, eighteen sheep, and a bull managed to swim ashore." In the heyday of river traffic (up to the 1920s) packets and showboats called at Clifton. As roads replaced rivers for transportation, Clifton vied for a bridge over the Kentucky but lost out to Tyrone, a few miles upriver.

7.3 Cross a creek.
Look to the right to see a small bridge resting on stone piers. Gear down now, as the climb out of the gorge starts just ahead. The climb lasts 0.7 mile at an almost constant grade.

This is as good a time as any to compare gorge riding to mountain riding. The Bluegrass offers lots of the former and none of the latter. The two kinds of riding require much the same skills, but different attitudes. Mountain riders climb first and coast later. Gorge riders do just the opposite. Mountain riding is like saving money for your vacation. You sweat and save for a long time, then spend it all in a glorious week in Paris. In contrast, gorge riding is like taking a vacation on borrowed money. You enjoy yourself first, then have to scrimp for months as you pay back the loan. This may explain why Bluegrass residents are more famous for spending money than saving it. It's something to think about as you grind up the Clifton hill.

Bourbon distilleries have a long tradition in Kentucky.

8.8 Left on Hippe-Agee Road.

9.3 Right on Watts Ferry Road.

9.9 Left on Germany Road.
This road leads to the Buckley Wildlife Sanctuary, and you must backtrack to this point to resume the loop. Even if you don't intend to visit the sanctuary, I urge you to take this road. It runs along a ridge with superb views.

10.4 Keep straight where an unmarked road (Shore Acres Road) forks left. The correct route is marked NO OUTLET.
Don't turn left here, as I once did when traveling without a map, unless you relish another steep climb out of the Kentucky River Gorge.

10.7 Pass Macedonia Baptist Church.
The road crests here, and you can look far off to the north and east. If the air is even just fairly clear, you can make out some of the big buildings in Frankfort.

11.2 Left into the Buckley Wildlife Sanctuary.

11.4 Turn around at the gravel parking lot.
The Buckley Sanctuary, run by the Audubon Society, has a bird blind and walking trails. Admission costs three dollars, payable by dropping your money into the wishing well. Leave the way you came.

11.7 Right on Germany Road as you leave the wildlife sanctuary.

13.0 Left on Watts Ferry Road.
Now you are back on the loop.

13.2 Straight as Watts Ferry Road joins KY 1964.

14.1 Right on KY 1659.
Millville Community Park is located at the junction, sandwiched between KY 1659 and Glenn's Creek. The park looks a bit run down, but the picnic tables offer a welcome respite. Note the his-and-hers outhouses.
　　For the next mile or so the road closely parallels Glenn's Creek. It's a pretty creek any time of year, but if you want to see it at its best, come on a sunny winter day when the trees are bare and the stream runs high with snowmelt.

15.1 Pass Labrot and Graham Distillery.
They've been making bourbon on this spot since 1812. Tours are available.

15.9 Keep right at the fork, staying on KY 1659.

16.7 Cross Glenn's Creek.
From here to mile 17.5 you can engage in some industrial archeology without leaving your bicycle saddle. A long-abandoned rail line parallels the road. Look for it first on the left side, then on the right. It's most obvious at mile 17.3 where the road again crosses Glenn's Creek and you can see the eroded piers of the former railroad bridge.

17.7 Cross Steele Road.

21.7 Enter the outskirts of Versailles.
Fine old houses line the street, here called Elm. The rich soil of the surrounding countryside made Versailles a prosperous town in the 19th century. Residents used their wealth to build impressive houses, many of which remain today—not just on Elm Street, but all around the downtown area.

22.3 Cross rough railroad tracks.

22.4 Right on Main Street.
Downtown Versailles is just ahead. The commercial center has moved east to the US 60 Bypass, but downtown still looks healthy—at least by 21st-century standards. Several eateries tempt the hungry cyclist, including an old-fashioned soda fountain and a barbecue joint.

The courthouse dates from 1970, but from its style you might take it to be much older. It's the fourth courthouse to stand here. The first, made of logs, was built in 1790 and cost $22.50. Courthouse prices have risen since then. The latest edition set the taxpayers of Woodford County back $1.1 million.

22.7 Right on Rose Hill Avenue, and then right again into the public parking lot to end the ride.

Bicycle Shops

None closer than Lexington.

Lodging

The Rose Hill Inn Bed & Breakfast (859-873-5957) stands on Rose Hill Avenue a few steps from the ride's starting point. For motels and hotels, head to Lexington or Frankfort.

10

Camp Nelson

- **DISTANCE:** 23.0 miles
- **HIGHLIGHTS:** The Palisades, Kentucky River bridges, Camp Nelson, and one of the best back roads in all the Bluegrass

The tour is harder than its 23-mile length implies. The terrain near the Kentucky River is all ravines and ridges, and the roads there seem to cut right across the drainage pattern. The result is a roller-coaster ride of short, steep grades.

If you want a longer ride, it's possible to combine this tour with Ride 12. Do Ride 12 first, but when you get to mile 27.2 continue straight on Main Street instead of turning left on Longview Drive, which will put you at mile 1.0 of this tour.

DIRECTIONS FOR THE RIDE

The ride starts in Nicholasville at the City–County Park. (I hope the officials didn't pay a consultant to come up with that name.) To reach the park from downtown Nicholasville, head south on Main Street. Turn left on Longview Drive, across from Kroger, and drive to the end. Park near the Parks and Recreation Office, which has public toilets (summer only).

0.0 Head out on Park Drive.

0.3 Straight as Park Drive becomes Longview Drive.

0.6 Stay on Longview Drive as it turns right, then left.

1.0 Left on Main Street.

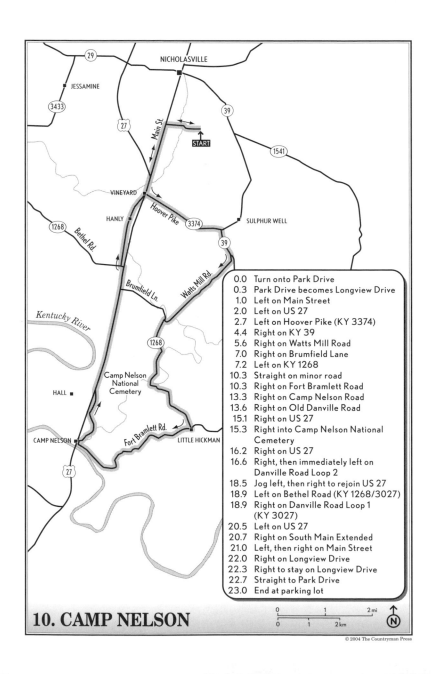

NICHOLASVILLE

JESSAMINE

29

3433

27

39

1541

Main St.

START

VINEYARD

HANLY

Hoover Pike

3374

SULPHUR WELL

1268

Bethel Rd.

39

Brumfield Ln.

Watts Mill Rd.

Kentucky River

1268

Camp Nelson
National
Cemetery

HALL

CAMP NELSON

27

Fort Bramlett Rd.

LITTLE HICKMAN

0.0	Turn onto Park Drive
0.3	Park Drive becomes Longview Drive
1.0	Left on Main Street
2.0	Left on US 27
2.7	Left on Hoover Pike (KY 3374)
4.4	Right on KY 39
5.6	Right on Watts Mill Road
7.0	Right on Brumfield Lane
7.2	Left on KY 1268
10.3	Straight on minor road
10.3	Right on Fort Bramlett Road
13.3	Right on Camp Nelson Road
13.6	Right on Old Danville Road
15.1	Right on US 27
15.3	Right into Camp Nelson National Cemetery
16.2	Right on US 27
16.6	Right, then immediately left on Danville Road Loop 2
18.5	Jog left, then right to rejoin US 27
18.9	Left on Bethel Road (KY 1268/3027)
18.9	Right on Danville Road Loop 1 (KY 3027)
20.5	Left on US 27
20.7	Right on South Main Extended
21.0	Left, then right on Main Street
22.0	Right on Longview Drive
22.3	Right to stay on Longview Drive
22.7	Straight to Park Drive
23.0	End at parking lot

10. CAMP NELSON

0   1   2 mi

0   1   2 km

N

Just north of this spot is a busy commercial district with a supermarket and several restaurants. If you need supplies for your trip, stock up now. You will pass no more stores till you return here near the end of the ride. Expect heavy traffic for the next mile.

2.0 Left on US 27, a four-lane divided highway with a wide, paved shoulder.

2.7 Left on Hoover Pike (KY 3374).
At mile 4.1 the road runs along a well-built dry-laid stone wall. Bluegrass residents call it a rock fence.

4.4 Right on KY 36 at the T-junction.
Now the roller-coaster hills begin.

5.6 Right on Watts Mill Road.

7.0 Right on Brumfield Lane (unmarked).

7.2 Left on KY 1268 (unmarked).

8.1 Start the descent into the Hickman Creek Valley.
Don't go so fast that you miss the view. Cross the creek at mile 8.8.

10.3 Straight on a minor road as KY 1268 turns left. Turn right on Fort Bramlett Road just a few yards past the junction where you left KY 1268.
You are in for a treat now, because Fort Bramlett Road is a back road among back roads. It winds for almost 3 miles through steep, wooded country. Then it drops down into the Hickman Creek Valley, where it runs along a narrow strip of land between the stream and limestone cliffs. It's paved, but only just. The pavement is one skimpy lane wide, and some sections are covered with loose gravel. I assume motorists use Fort Bramlett Road, but I have yet to encounter one there.

13.3 Right on Camp Nelson Road (unmarked) at the T-junction, and cross Hickman Creek.
You are now in the Kentucky River Gorge.

13.5 Pass under the high-level bridge where US 27 crosses the gorge.

13.6 Right on Old Danville Road (unmarked).
But don't turn right just yet. Park your bike and explore on foot, because there's a lot to see here. On your left is the steel truss bridge that used to carry US 27 across the Kentucky River. Engineers condemned it and closed it to motor traffic in 1997.

Camp Nelson National Cemetery.

It's still open to pedestrians, however. Climb over the guardrail and walk out on the bridge. Look right for a superb view of the Kentucky River Palisades. The gorge is at its narrowest here. Look left to see the bridge that replaced the one you are standing on, as well as the ruins of the bridge that came before.

The stone piers upstream supported the Hickman Bridge, a covered bridge completed in 1838. It was a monster—241 feet long and two lanes wide, the longest timber cantilever bridge in America—and it carried traffic well into the car age. State officials ruled the Hickman unsafe in 1926, and ferries ran night and day to keep the road link open while the next bridge—the one you are standing on—was built.

The newest crossing, the Loyd Murphy Memorial Bridge, carries four lanes of US 27 high above the river. It does its job well, but you don't see it on postcards or calendars. In contrast, think what a prize Kentucky would have today had the old covered bridge been preserved. And $30,000 would have done the job.

Returning to the riverbank, you find yourself in Camp Nelson—more or less. Camp Nelson has great historic importance, but as an actual place on the ground it's hard to pin down. It started out as a Civil War camp that sprawled over the plain atop the palisades. Later, the name attached itself to two riverbank communities near the mouth of Hickman Creek—first on the north side of the river in Jessamine County and then on south side in Garrard.

Camp Nelson's greatest fame, and greatest shame, came during the Civil War. The fame arose from the camp's role as a recruiting station and training center for African Americans, who could escape slavery by joining the Union army. The shame came about because Kentucky, though loyal to the Union, remained a slave state throughout the war. Men could free themselves by enlisting, but their wives and children remained at risk. Many of those dependents took refuge at Camp Nelson. In November 1864 the army kicked some 400 refugees out into the freezing weather. Though they were later allowed back in, at least 102 died. Overall, about a third of the refugees who entered Camp Nelson did not leave alive.

13.7 Pass through a tunnel under US 27, and start the climb out of the Kentucky River Gorge.

15.1 Right on US 27.
The gray, military-looking buildings across the highway are whiskey warehouses.

15.3 Right into Camp Nelson National Cemetery.
This is the final resting place for over 5,000 Union soldiers, along with veterans of later wars.

15.7 Turn around at the loop inside the cemetery.
Bear right as you ride out and stop at the hilltop where the flagpole stands. It offers a good view of the cemetery and the surrounding farmland.

16.2 Right on US 27 as you leave the cemetery.

16.6 Right, and immediately left, on Danville Road Loop 2.
This is the old US 27, running alongside its four-lane replacement. Pass the Camp Nelson Heritage Park at mile 16.9.

18.5 Jog left at the red church, then right to rejoin US 27.

18.9 Left on Bethel Road (KY 1268/3027).

18.9 Right on Danville Road Loop 1 (KY 3027). Now you're back on old US 27.

20.5 Left on US 27.

20.7 Right on South Main Extended.

21.0 Left then right on Main Street. The Nicholasville city limit sign is in view.

22.0 Right on Longview Drive. A sign points to the City-County Park.

22.3 Right, staying on Longview Drive.

22.7 Straight to Park Drive, and into the park.

23.0 End at the parking lot.

Bicycle Shops

None closer than Lexington.

Lodging

None along the route, but there are several motels on the north side of Nicholasville.

11

Licking River

- **DISTANCE:** 26.5 miles
- **HIGHLIGHTS:** Kincaid Lake State Park, the town of Falmouth, and views of the Licking River

The Licking River is one of Kentucky's great waterways. It is 320 miles long and drains a big part of the Bluegrass, along with much of Eastern Kentucky. Interesting things have happened here.

In 1780, during the American Revolution, some 600 British and Indian fighters under Henry Byrd (sometimes spelled Bird) came up the river's main stem, looking for trouble. They landed at the forks, near present-day Falmouth. From there they marched overland, hauling two artillery pieces, to attack American settlements at Ruddell's Station and Martin's Station. Both settlements fell; Martin's Station surrendered without a fight. What happened next wasn't pretty. About 20 Americans were killed on the spot. Survivors were marched north to Detroit, where they remained captive till the war's end.

The Licking has also seen happy, peaceful times. In 1942 Harlan Hubbard and his wife-to-be, Anna Eikenhout, spent nine days paddling a canoe down the river, camping each night on shore. They put in at West Liberty in Morgan County, far upriver in Eastern Kentucky, and floated down to Covington where the river meets the Ohio. Harlan cooked their meals, while Anna read aloud from her favorite books. The Licking River trip cemented their relationship, which led to marriage the following year and to a long life together.

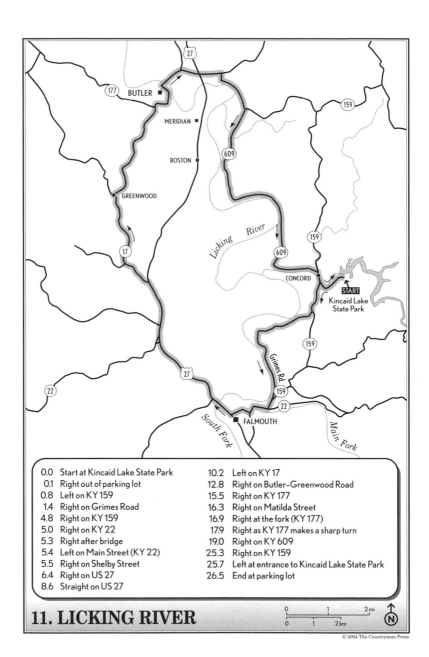

0.0	Start at Kincaid Lake State Park	
0.1	Right out of parking lot	
0.8	Left on KY 159	
1.4	Right on Grimes Road	
4.8	Right on KY 159	
5.0	Right on KY 22	
5.3	Right after bridge	
5.4	Left on Main Street (KY 22)	
5.5	Right on Shelby Street	
6.4	Right on US 27	
8.6	Straight on US 27	
10.2	Left on KY 17	
12.8	Right on Butler–Greenwood Road	
15.5	Right on KY 177	
16.3	Right on Matilda Street	
16.9	Right at the fork (KY 177)	
17.9	Right as KY 177 makes a sharp turn	
19.0	Right on KY 609	
25.3	Right on KY 159	
25.7	Left at entrance to Kincaid Lake State Park	
26.5	End at parking lot	

11. LICKING RIVER

0   1   2 mi
0   1   2 km

N

The trip also foreshadowed a more famous adventure on the Ohio and Mississippi Rivers, told by Hubbard in his book *Shantyboat*. After their epic travels, Harlan and Anna settled down in Trimble County, where they built a house with their own hands and followed a simple but satisfying lifestyle without electricity or much in the way of modern conveniences.

In addition to his accomplishments as boatman, painter, writer, and exemplar of the simple life, Harlan Hubbard was a bicyclist. He rode many miles over the Kentucky back roads on his English three-speed. That's something to think about the next time you're debating whether to drop a few hundred dollars on the latest bike gizmo from Shimano or Campagnolo.

DIRECTIONS FOR THE RIDE

0.0 Start at Kincaid Lake State Park, at the parking lot near the boat ramp. The park lies in Pendleton County, northeast of Falmouth.
Kincaid Lake is artificial, like all lakes in the Bluegrass. It covers 183 acres and dates from 1961. Fishing is popular here, and if you want to explore the lake you can rent a rowboat or small motorboat at the park. Motors are limited to 10 horsepower, keeping this lake more tranquil than some others. The state park includes a big campground with good tenting sites, as well as a few miles of hiking trails. The hiking here is surprisingly good, though you can't go far. One trail crosses a wooden suspension bridge.

0.1 Right on the park road as you leave the parking lot.
A left here would take you to the park campground (closed in winter).

0.8 Left on KY 159 at the T-junction.

1.4 Right on Grimes Road (unmarked). You pass a black barn on the left just before the turn.
Though paved, Grimes Road is rough and very narrow. If you hate that kind of road, stay on KY 159 and rejoin the route where Grimes Road meets 159 again at mile 4.8. You'll miss some close river views and you'll have to climb a big hill, but the trade-off is a vista of Falmouth from the hilltop. Both options are good.

2.6 Expect very rough pavement here.

4.8 Right on KY 159.

5.0 Right on KY 22 at the T-junction.

5.3 Cross the Licking River on a bright blue truss bridge.

5.3 Right immediately after crossing the bridge.

5.4 Left on Main Street at the four-way stop sign. You are still on KY 22.
Downtown Falmouth lies ahead. The town got its charter in 1793, but the settlement may go back as far as 1780. It used to be called Forks of the Licking, an accurate name since it lies where the Licking River's two main branches form the main stem.

Falmouth's citizens must have mixed feelings about the Licking River. The river made their city, but more than once it came close to breaking it. Floods caused extensive damage four times in the 20th century. For years, there has been talk about building a big dam to reduce floods, but the Licking remains untamed.

5.5 Right on Shelby Street.

5.7 Cross railroad tracks and enter a middle-class residential neighborhood.
A bed & breakfast is located on the right at mile 5.9.

6.4 Right on US 27 at the T-junction.
Several stores and restaurants are close by.

6.5 Cross the South Fork of the Licking River.
Though smaller than the main branch you crossed on the way into Falmouth, this is still a good-sized stream. It drains much of the Inner Bluegrass, with tributaries reaching as far south as Winchester. Beyond the river, US 27 starts a steep climb out of the Licking Valley.

8.6 Straight on US 27 as KY 22 branches left.

10.2 Left on KY 17.
The land here slopes steeply, with V-shaped valleys in all directions, but the road stays level as it follows the ridgeline. The views here are superb.

12.8 Right on Butler–Greenwood Road in the village of Greenwood (no services).
At mile 13.1 the road starts down, leaving the ridge for the Licking Valley.

15.5 Right on KY 177.

16.0 Cross under a railroad through a small tunnel and enter the town of Butler. The road becomes Mill Street in town, where it passes two restaurants.

Butler is not an old town by Bluegrass standards. It developed after the railroad came through in 1852. From 1871 to 1937 you could cross the Licking River here on a huge covered bridge, claimed by some to be the world's biggest. The great flood of 1937 wrecked it, and today we have to settle for an ordinary steel bridge.

Butler used to be called Fourth Lock, for a lock and dam on the river. Nineteenth-century entrepreneurs hoped to open the Licking River to steamboat navigation by installing locks and dams, as they were doing on the Kentucky and other rivers. The plan did not work out, however. The river turned out to be more suitable for floating logs down to Cincinnati than for steamboating. Today the river sees little boat traffic of any kind.

Back in the 1800s, plans to dam and canalize the rivers of America were as common as Internet start-ups at the turn of the 21st century—and no more successful, on average. In the Bluegrass, visionaries imagined chains of dams and locks on the Kentucky, Licking, and Salt Rivers, opening the whole region to steamboats. Only the Kentucky River plans amounted to much, and even there the hoped-for traffic never materialized.

16.3 Right on Matilda Street and cross the Licking River.

The Licking River near Butler.

Bicycling is great, but the best way to explore the Licking River is in a canoe. If you want to try that, Butler is the place to start. Thaxton's Licking River Canoe Rentals is based nearby at 33 Hornbeck Road (859-472-2000) and can help with transportation to and from the canoe landings. Several canoe routes are available, depending on water levels. When the water is high, the upper parts of the river (above Falmouth) offer good canoeing. In low water the main stem right here in Butler is your best bet.

16.9 Right at the fork, staying on KY 177 as KY 3149 heads left.

17.3 Cross US 27.
There are two convenience stores at the intersection.

17.9 Right as KY 177 makes a sharp turn.
Less than a quarter mile ahead the road swings close to the Licking River, offering a good view of the floodplain.

19.0 Right on KY 609.

25.3 Right on KY 159 at the T-junction in the village of Concord (no services).
The Pendleton County Wool Festival is held here every year on the first weekend of October.

25.7 Left at the entrance to Kincaid Lake State Park.

26.4 Left into the boat-ramp area, unless you are staying at the park campground. In that case, keep straight.

26.5 End at the parking lot.

Bicycle Shops

None on the tour, or even close to it.

Lodging

You can camp at Kincaid Lake State Park, within steps of the tour's start. If you prefer to sleep indoors, head to a bed & breakfast in Falmouth or Butler.

High Bridge

- **DISTANCE:** 28.2 miles
- **HIGHLIGHTS:** The High Bridge, the Kentucky River Palisades, a river look, and the towns of Nicholasville and Wilmore

Part of this route runs beside Jessamine Creek. It's one of the prettiest streams in the Bluegrass, and that's saying something. Jessamine County was named for the creek. The creek was probably named for the jessamine flower, which grew nearby—what most people today call jasmine. Some people tell a more interesting, though probably fictitious, story about the naming of the creek. A Scottish surveyor, James Douglass, visited the area in the days of Indian raids. His daughter Jessamine came with him. Indians tomahawked little Jessamine next to the creek, which was named in her honor.

This ride covers a good cross section of Jessamine County, including farmland on the Bluegrass plain, steep country near the Kentucky River, and the two biggest towns, Nicholasville and Wilmore. Jessamine is a blue-collar kind of county, and you can see that in town and country alike. Nicholasville, the county seat and by far the biggest town, is full of working-class bungalows and duplexes. Many residents commute to jobs in Lexington, but some work at factories and warehouses in town. The farms of Jessamine County—at least in the area of this tour—tend to be workaday places that raise more cattle and corn than thoroughbreds.

For an even better look at Jessamine County, combine this tour

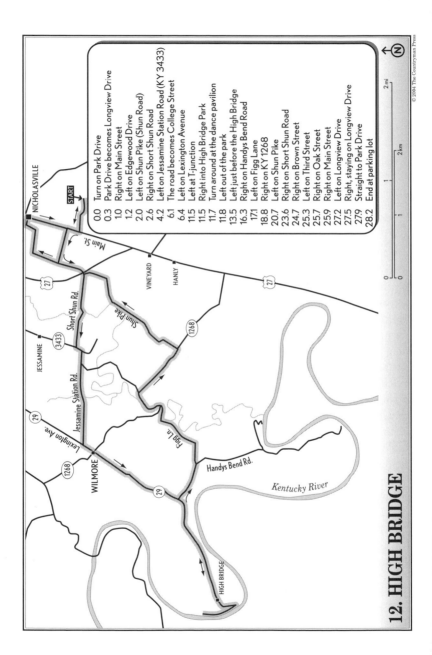

12. HIGH BRIDGE

© 2004 The Countryman Press

0.0	Turn on Park Drive
0.3	Park Drive becomes Longview Drive
1.0	Right on Main Street
1.2	Left on Edgewood Drive
2.0	Left on Shun Pike (Shun Road)
2.6	Right on Short Shun Road
4.2	Left on Jessamine Station Road (KY 3433)
6.1	The road becomes College Street
6.4	Left on Lexington Avenue
11.5	Left at T-junction
11.5	Right into High Bridge Park
11.7	Turn around at the dance pavilion
11.8	Left out of the park
13.5	Left just before the High Bridge
16.3	Right on Handys Bend Road
17.1	Left on Figg Lane
18.8	Right on KY 1268
20.7	Left on Shun Pike
23.6	Right on Short Shun Road
24.7	Right on Brown Street
25.3	Left on Third Street
25.7	Right on Oak Street
25.9	Right on Main Street
27.2	Left on Longview Drive
27.5	Right, staying on Longview Drive
27.9	Straight to Park Drive
28.2	End at parking lot

with Ride 10. Do this one first, but when you reach mile 27.2, continue straight on Main Street instead of turning left on Longview Drive, which puts you at mile 1.0 of Ride 10.

DIRECTIONS FOR THE RIDE

The ride starts in Nicholasville at the City–County Park. To reach the park from downtown Nicholasville, head south on Main Street. Turn left on Longview Drive, across from Kroger, and drive to the end. Park near the Parks and Recreation Office, which has public toilets (summer only).

0.0 Head out on Park Drive.

0.3 Straight as Park Drive becomes Longview Drive.

0.6 Stay on Longview Drive as it turns right then left.

1.0 Right on Main Street.
You are now entering a busy retail district, with a supermarket, Mexican restaurant, and several fast-food places.

1.2 Left on Edgewood Drive, which runs through a typical Nicholasville neighborhood of small duplex houses.

2.0 Left on Shun Pike.
The sign says SHUN ROAD, but that's not the original name and it doesn't even make sense. The name goes back to the days when Kentucky was full of privately owned toll roads called turnpikes, or pikes for short. People too poor or too cheap to pay tolls sought routes that bypassed the tollgates. Those alternative roads were called shun pikes because they let travelers shun the turnpikes.

Nowadays, the term has become a verb with a slightly different meaning. To shunpike is to travel on back roads instead of the interstates and limited-access turnpikes. By that definition, we cyclists almost always ride on a shun pike.

2.6 Right on Short Shun Road.

4.2 Left on Jessamine Station Road (KY 3433, unmarked) at the T-junction.

6.1 Cross over railroad tracks and see Wilmore ahead. The road becomes College Street.

6.4 Left on Lexington Avenue.

The High Bridge.

A statue of Bishop Francis Asbury on his horse stands opposite a convenience store. Asbury was an early leader of the Methodist Church who made many trips to Kentucky, starting in 1790. Wilmore's dominant feature is the liberal-arts college that bears Asbury's name.

6.6 Cross Main Street.
A grocery store and a Subway are within view here. Downtown Wilmore is a couple of blocks to the left.

8.2 Cross over the Norfolk Southern railroad tracks, which run through a deep cut.
This is the same rail line that crosses the Kentucky River at High Bridge.

11.0 Cross under the railroad tracks and enter the village of High Bridge.

11.5 Left at the T-junction and cross under the bridge.

11.5 Right into High Bridge Park.

A century ago folks from Lexington and even Cincinnati rode the train here for picnics and parties. In those days, wooden stairs led down the cliffs to the river-bank. The park fell into disuse and disrepair, but has just recently been fixed up. The stairs are gone, but the park now includes a lookout pier—sort of a half bridge—with an unmatched view of the Kentucky River Gorge.

11.7 Turn around at the dance pavilion.
Before you leave the park, walk out to the scenic overlook. Below you is the conflu-ence of the Kentucky and Dix Rivers. The High Bridge is to your right.

Bridge construction at this spot began in the 1850s. John A. Roebling, the engineer who went on to design the Brooklyn Bridge, built towers for a suspension bridge. It would have been magnificent, but the financial panic of 1857 stopped the job. The bridge that spanned the gorge two decades later was of a completely different design—a steel cantilever by Charles Shaler Smith. It was completely rebuilt in 1911, turning it into the heavy bridge that still carries long Norfolk Southern freight trains across the gorge. Cantilever bridges are known more for ruggedness than grace, and this one is true to type. It's not beautiful, but it looks like it will last a thousand years.

Though it was always a railroad bridge, local people used to walk across. No doubt some still do, but there's a fine to pay if you get caught.

11.8 Left as you leave the park. Pass under the bridge.

11.9 Straight at the junction just beyond the bridge.
There is a steep downgrade as you descend into the gorge.

12.4 Straight between the stone gateposts at the bottom of the hill.
Ahead is Lock Number 7 in a park-like setting. The lockkeeper lived here, and I envy him. This lock, along with all the other locks above Frankfort, has been closed for several years. The Army Corps of Engineers gave up on the locks after com-mercial barge traffic disappeared. The state government ran the locks for a couple of years, but never invested enough money to keep them going. Their future is unclear. Unlike some of the other closed locks, Number 7 is still in good shape and looks ready to go. You can walk out on the lock gates and picture the workboats locking through, the barge hands sweating and swearing as they work their boats in and out.

12.7 Turn around at lock.
A grotto in the limestone cliff holds a spring, fitted with a long pipe that makes

drawing water easy. Conventional wisdom holds that you should never drink from an unapproved water source without purifying it first. So I won't advise you to fill your water bottle here. However, I will say that I never fail to top up here myself, and I've seen locals filling drums to take home.

13.5 Left at the top of hill, just before the High Bridge.

16.3 Right on Handy's Bend Road.

17.1 Left on Figg Lane.
After crossing a hill or two, Figg Lane reaches Jessamine Creek, which here flows through a mini-gorge that branches off from the Kentucky River Gorge.

18.8 Right on KY 1268.

18.9 Cross Jessamine Creek on a narrow bridge near an old mill dam.
The road continues beside the creek for a few hundred feet before climbing out of the mini-gorge.

19.5 Right as KY 1268 makes a hard right turn at the junction with Frankfort Ford Road.

20.7 Left on Shun Pike.
The road crosses two creeks. The first is Town Creek. The second is our old friend Jessamine Creek, which looks quite different here from the stream down in the mini-gorge.

23.6 Right on Short Shun Road (unmarked) at the T-junction.

24.2 Cross Edgewood Drive.
If you want to miss downtown Nicholasville, turn right here and right again at the first traffic light, where you will rejoin the route at mile 26.9.

24.7 Right on Brown Street.

25.3 Left on Third Street.

25.7 Right on Oak Street.

25.9 Right on Main Street.
Downtown Nicholasville, which occupies the next few blocks, has not fared as well as some other Kentucky downtowns. Wal-Mart came early to Nicholasville and sucked most of the retail business out to the north end. Some downtowns have

remade themselves with antiques shops and trendy restaurants, but that hasn't quite worked here.

27.2 Left on Longview Drive. A sign points to the City-County Park.

27.5 Right, staying on Longview Drive.

27.9 Straight to Park Drive and into the park.

28.2 End at the parking lot.

Bicycle Shops

None closer than Lexington.

Lodging

None on the route, but there are several motels on the north side of Nicholasville.

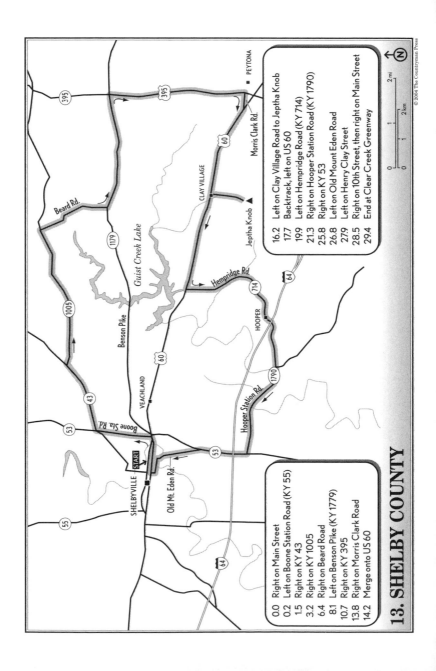

13. SHELBY COUNTY

© 2004 The Countryman Press

N

0.0	Right on Main Street
0.2	Left on Boone Station Road (KY 55)
1.5	Right on KY 43
3.2	Right on KY 1005
6.4	Right on Beard Road
8.1	Left on Benson Pike (KY 1779)
10.7	Right on KY 395
13.8	Right on Morris Clark Road
14.2	Merge onto US 60

16.2	Left on Clay Village Road to Jeptha Knob
17.7	Backtrack, left on US 60
19.9	Left on Hempridge Road (KY 714)
21.3	Right on Hooper Station Road (KY 1790)
25.8	Right on KY 53
26.8	Left on Old Mount Eden Road
27.9	Left on Henry Clay Street
28.5	Right on 10th Street, then right on Main Street
29.4	End at Clear Creek Greenway

Shelby County

- **DISTANCE:** 29.4 miles
- **HIGHLIGHTS:** Downtown Shelbyville, big farms, and Jeptha Knob

Jeptha Knob dominates the eastern part of Shelby County, and is visible for miles in all directions. At 1,188 feet, its summit is the highest point in the whole Bluegrass region, but that's just the start of what is unique about it. If geologists are right about how the Bluegrass was formed, Jeptha Knob should not exist.

The Bluegrass is a land of valleys, not peaks. It started out flat, as sediments built up at the bottom of a shallow sea. As the sea receded and the land gently rose, erosion from flowing water created valleys and gorges. Due to that history, the region's most dramatic features are holes, not hills. High ground is spread out and consists of what is left of the original flat plain. The steepest grades don't occur near the high ground, as in a mountain range, but in the gorges.

That's all just basic geology, but Jeptha Knob defies it. The knob is, without doubt, a peak. How did it get there? Geologists have two theories about that.

The older theory, endorsed by a roadside marker in Clay Village, calls Jeptha Knob a crypto-volcano, which is a volcano that tried to form but didn't quite erupt. The land bulged, but no lava and ash came out.

The newer and more likely theory holds that a meteorite strike created the knob. It would have taken a big rock—one with the mass of a battleship. It's not pleasant to imagine what such a strike would mean today, but this one happened millions of years ago.

Except for Jeptha Knob, Shelby County's terrain typifies the Outer Bluegrass: a gently rolling plain punctuated with creeks, some of which flow in deep valleys. The land supports farming on a larger scale than seen in most other Bluegrass counties. Big fields and dairy farms give the landscape an almost midwestern look. Shelby County's farmers grow a variety of crops, but are known for their alfalfa.

DIRECTIONS FOR THE RIDE

The ride starts at the Clear Creek Greenway Park on Main Street (US 60) in Shelbyville, about half a mile east of the courthouse. If the few parking spots are taken, park downtown instead.

0.0 Right on Main Street as you leave the park.

0.2 Left on Boone Station Road (KY 55), which has a paved shoulder.
A shopping center here has a supermarket and a few restaurants. Stop if you need anything for the trip, since stores are few and far between on this route.

1.3 Cross over Mulberry Creek and a set of railroad tracks.

1.5 Right on KY 43.

3.2 Right on KY 1005 and cross railroad tracks.

6.4 Right on Beard Road.
Get ready for a couple of steep grades as the road crosses two creeks.

8.1 Left on Benson Pike (KY 1779, unmarked) at a T-junction.

10.7 Right on KY 395.

13.8 Right on Morris Clark Road in the village of Peytona.

14.2 Merge onto US 60.
It would be nice if this road were wider or less busy, but it's the only public road going to Jeptha Knob, and you don't want to miss that.

16.2 Left on Clay Village Road (unmarked), a feeder road that parallels US 60.

A farm building at the top of Jeptha Knob.

16.3 Left on Jeptha Knob Road.

16.9 Left onto a rutted dirt road.
Things get tricky here, because public access to Jeptha Knob is limited. The peak is in private hands, leased to communications companies that have erected radio towers there. The paved road continues to the top, but a locked gate blocks the way. The dirt road at mile 16.9 provides an alternate route up. There's a gate on this road, too, but I've never seen it closed. It's the steepest road I've seen anywhere in the Bluegrass, and rough to boot. If you ride a mountain bike with low gears and big tires, you may be able to pedal up. Otherwise, it's a 0.1-mile walk.

17.0 Turn around at the radio tower.
This part of Jeptha Knob offers good views to the north (showing the farmland you recently rode through) and east. From here you can explore the summit on foot. There are actually several peaks, each topped with at least one radio tower. It's hard to tell which one is the highest. The summit includes some flat land that used to be farmed.

17.1 Right onto a paved road.

17.7 Left on Clay Village Road, then left on US 60.

19.9 Left on Hempridge Road (KY 714).

21.3 Right on Hooper Station Road (KY 1790).

22.3 Cross railroad tracks at an angle.

22.6 Cross over I-64.

25.8 Right on KY 53, which has a paved shoulder, and then cross I-64.
The interstate junction hosts a Holiday Inn Express and a few convenience stores.

26.8 Left on Old Mount Eden Road, across from the Ken-Tex Barbecue.
The road bends sharply left at mile 27.7, where you'll find the old Marcardin Inn, a bed & breakfast.

27.8 Cross Clear Creek and enter the built-up part of Shelbyville.
The town park here has a paved boat ramp just for canoes.

27.9 Left on Henry Clay Street.
Check out the unusual architecture of the Bethel A.M.E. Church.

28.5 Right on 10th Street, then right on Main Street after one block. Downtown Shelbyville lies ahead.

Shelbyville looks healthy and prosperous. It's just the right distance from Louisville—close enough to attract commuters, but far enough away to maintain a distinct identity. The town is known for its Christmas decorations. That won't count for much if you arrive in midsummer, but the town is worth a visit in any season. The courthouse dates from 1912 and is on the National Register. Science Hill Inn, a restaurant in a former girls' school, cooks up traditional Bluegrass meals.

29.4 End the ride at Clear Creek Greenway.

Bicycle Shops

The nearest are in Louisville.

Lodging

Holiday Inn Express (502-647-0109) is at mile 25.8 and Marcardin Inn (502-633-2568) at mile 26.8. You can also camp at the Clear Creek Park on Shelbyville's north side.

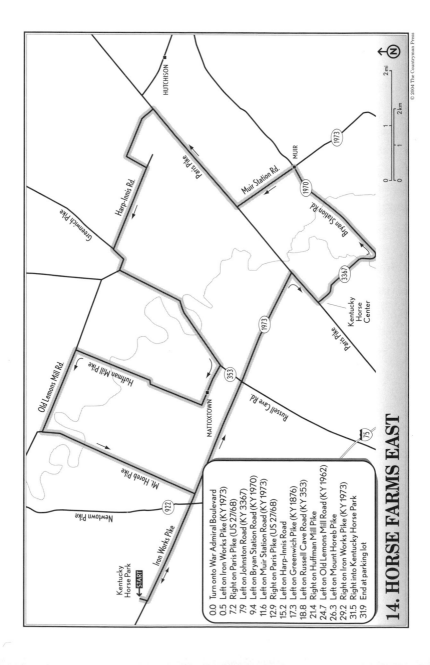

14. HORSE FARMS EAST

0.0 Turn onto War Admiral Boulevard
0.5 Left on Iron Works Pike (KY 1973)
7.2 Right on Paris Pike (US 27/68)
7.9 Left on Johnston Road (KY 3367)
9.4 Left on Bryan Station Road (KY 1970)
11.6 Left on Muir Station Road (KY 1973)
12.9 Right on Paris Pike (US 27/68)
15.2 Left on Harp-Innis Road
17.3 Left on Greenwich Pike (KY 1876)
18.8 Left on Russell Cave Road (KY 353)
21.4 Right on Huffman Mill Pike
24.7 Left on Old Lemons Mill Road (KY 1962)
26.3 Left on Mount Horeb Pike
29.2 Right on Iron Works Pike (KY 1973)
31.5 Right into Kentucky Horse Park
31.9 End at parking lot

© 2004 The Countryman Press

14

Horse Farms East

- **DISTANCE:** 31.9 miles
- **HIGHLIGHTS:** Magnificent horse farms, the Kentucky Horse Park, and the Jot 'Em Down country store

This tour loops through the rich horse-farm country north and east of Lexington. Several rides in this book pass horse farms, but this one offers the densest concentration. When folks in Tokyo or Tehran picture the Bluegrass, this is the landscape they have in mind. The fields are green and as neat as a golf course. The fences go on forever. And the horses look healthy and happy.

You may think of breeding and raising horse as a hobby—and in some places it is—but here in the heart of the Bluegrass it's an industry. It supports a surprisingly large number of people, most of them earning modest wages. You see few of those workers from the public roads, however. Most of the activity takes place deep within the farms, where networks of private roads connect barns, work-shops, and houses. It's not secret—some farms offer public tours—but it is somewhat hidden.

You can reach this ride by Lexington city bus, provided you don't mind cycling a few extra miles. Take the Number 2 (Newtown) bus to the north end of the line. Then ride north on Newtown Pike for 2.2 miles. Turn right when you reach Iron Works Pike, where you join the tour at mile 2.5.

DIRECTIONS FOR THE RIDE

This tour starts at the Kentucky Horse Park, where acres of free parking are available.

0.0 From the main parking lot, take War Admiral Boulevard toward the park entrance.

0.5 Left on Iron Works Pike (KY 1973).

0.9 Pass a campground entrance on the left.

2.2 Pass Spindletop Farm on the right.
Formerly a working horse farm, Spindletop is now used by the University of Kentucky for research. The farm is unusually treeless. Most days you can see the Lexington skyline (such as it is) in the distance.

2.5 Cross Newtown Pike (KY 922).

5.0 Cross Russell Cave Road.
The Jot 'Em Down Store at the corner has been selling beer and snacks to horse-farm hands since the Great Depression. If you remember the 1930s, or if you are a fan of old radio shows, you may recognize the store's name. Radio characters Lum and Abner ran the original, fictional Jot 'Em Down Store in a nightly comedy show.

Back then the real store on Russell Cave Road was called Terrell's Grocery. Some of its customers started calling the storekeepers Lum and Abner. Soon even the customers were taking the names of characters from the radio show. I imagine that similar things happened at country stores all over the place, but at Terrell's the process went further. The real Lum and Abner came to Lexington to buy horses. The actors heard about the store and paid it a visit, leaving a JOT 'EM DOWN STORE sign. And that has been the store's name ever since.

The store could have turned into a tourist trap over the years, selling souvenirs to folks who couldn't care less who Lum and Abner were. Thank goodness that didn't happen. Jot 'Em Down is still a normal store selling the locals normal stuff. The sign in front advertises Budweiser, not knickknacks.

6.0 Pass Spendthrift Farm on the right.

7.2 Right on Paris Pike (US 27/68).
This is the main highway connecting Lexington with Paris and points northeast. Before 2003 it was a crowded two-lane road with a reputation for fatal crashes.

Classic stone walls and modern horse-farm fences are common sights.

Some people wanted to widen it, but many others opposed the project because the road passed through such a scenic, historic landscape. The road wideners won. Don't they always?

But they did the job with more care than usual. Rock fences and fancy farm entrances were moved at great expense. Stabilized soil lets grass grow right up to the roadway edge. And guardrails are made of timber, not galvanized steel. All of this makes the road a delight for touring motorists.

Unfortunately, the road builders didn't do much for cyclists when they widened Paris Pike. They left about 18 inches of asphalt to the right of the paint stripe, but then ruined it for biking by cutting rumble strips into it. Cyclists must share the main travel lane with fast motor traffic. Still, it's a lot better than the old two-lane road. That was one scary ride.

7.9 Left on Johnston Road (KY 3367).
The Thoroughbred Center offers guided tours.

9.4 Left on Bryan Station Road (KY 1970).

11.6 Left on Muir Station Road (KY 1973).
A country store occupies the southwest corner of the intersection.

12.9 Right on Paris Pike (US 27/68).

14.4 Enter Bourbon County.
This county lent its name to the liquid gold that Kentucky still makes in abundance. Ironically, bourbon is no longer made in Bourbon County.

14.6 Pass Terry's Corner Store at the junction with Houston–Antioch Road.

15.2 Left on Harp–Innis Road.

16.1 Enter Fayette County.

17.3 Left on Greenwich Pike (KY 1876).

18.8 Left on Russell Cave Road (KY 353).

20.7 Cross North Elkhorn Creek.
Just ahead on the right is Russell Cave, visible from the road. Here the anti-slavery politician Cassius Marcellus Clay used his bowie knife on a would-be assassin.

21.4 Right on Huffman Mill Pike.
The huge Mount Brilliant Farm stretches northwest from this corner.

24.0 Cross North Elkhorn Creek again.

24.7 Left on Old Lemons Mill Road (KY 1962).

26.3 Left on Mount Horeb Pike.

29.2 Right on Iron Works Pike (KY 1973).
A pretty limestone church stands here. It's Presbyterian, like many rural churches in the Bluegrass.

29.4 Cross Newtown Pike (KY 922).

31.5 Right into Kentucky Horse Park.

31.9 End the ride at the parking lot.

Bicycle Shops

Dodds Cyclery, 1985 Harrodsburg Road, Lexington; 859-277-6013

Pedal Power, 401 South Upper Street, Lexington; 859-255-6408

Scheller's, 212 Woodland Avenue, Lexington; 859-233-1764

Vicious Cycle, Todds Road at Codell, Lexington; 859-263-7300

Lodging

Several hotels—Knights Inn (859-231-0232), Holiday Inn (859-233-0512), La Quinta (859-231-7551), and Four Points (859-259-1311)—are clustered 2 miles south of the route at Exit 115 on I-75. From there, you can head north 2.2 miles on Newtown Pike and join the tour at mile 2.5. The Kentucky Horse Park includes a big campground (closed in winter). Enter from Iron Works Pike, about half a mile east of the main park gate.

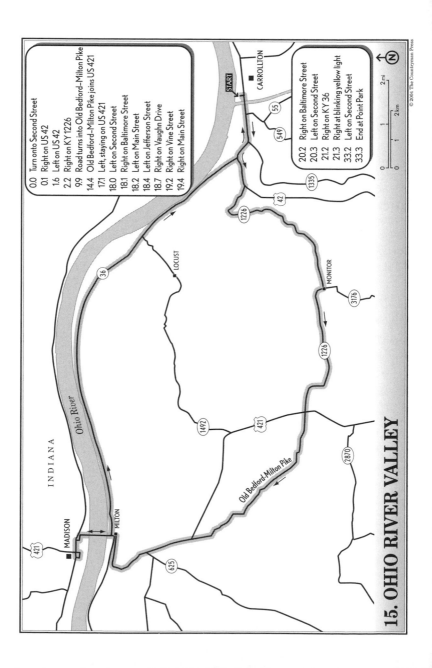

15. OHIO RIVER VALLEY

0.0	Turn onto Second Street
0.1	Right on US 42
1.6	Left on US 42
2.2	Right on KY 1226
9.9	Road turns into Old Bedford–Milton Pike
14.4	Old Bedford–Milton Pike joins US 421
17.1	Left, staying on US 421
18.0	Left on Second Street
18.1	Right on Baltimore Street
18.2	Left on Main Street
18.4	Left on Jefferson Street
18.7	Right on Vaughn Drive
19.2	Right on Vine Street
19.4	Right on Main Street

20.2	Right on Baltimore Street
20.3	Left on Second Street
21.2	Right on KY 36
21.3	Right at blinking yellow light
33.2	Left on Second Street
33.3	End at Point Park

© 2004 The Countryman Press

15

Ohio River Valley

- **DISTANCE:** 33.3 miles
- **HIGHLIGHTS:** River views and the Ohio River towns of Carrollton and Madison

The tour starts and ends in Carrollton, one of the prettiest Ohio River towns in Kentucky. It also goes to Madison, Indiana, which is the prettiest Ohio River town, period. The route takes the high road on the way to Madison, climbing Kings Ridge, and then takes the low road back, closely following the Ohio River.

The tour doesn't go through downtown Carrollton, but you can walk there from Point Park, the starting point. The town layout follows a plan seen in dozens of Kentucky's county seats. The courthouse stands on a square, surrounded by the downtown businesses. The difference in Carrollton is the presence of the mighty Ohio River, which flows close to the town center.

You must cross a long, somewhat intimidating bridge between Milton and Madison on this ride. On second thought, you don't actually have to cross it. You can simply turn around in Milton and still do most of the tour. But then you'll miss Madison, and that town is worth a look.

DIRECTIONS FOR THE RIDE

Start at Point Park in Carrollton. The park, which has picnic tables and rest rooms, lies at the west end of Main Street, a block north of US 42. It's a small, modest park, but this is an important place. The two greatest rivers of the Bluegrass—the Kentucky and Ohio—join here.

0.0 From the park, head away from the Ohio River on Second Street.

0.1 Right on US 42 and cross the Kentucky River.
Take the sidewalk across the bridge—not because the roadway isn't safe, but because you can easily stop to take in the view. During my last two visits, a paddle-wheel boat was tied up below the bridge.

0.5 Enter Prestonburg. Keep straight as KY 55 splits left.
The town has a store and a restaurant.

1.6 Left on US 42, which leaves the Ohio here to head inland.
The road goes up the narrow valley of the Little Kentucky River.

2.2 Right on KY 1226, which start climbing right away.
The steep grade tops out at mile 3.2, putting you on the top of Kings Ridge. The road keeps to the ridgeline for several miles.

6.1 Enter Trimble County.
Half a mile ahead the road crosses a treeless meadow, providing a great view. You can see far into Indiana.

Madison, Indiana, a beautiful little Ohio River town.

9.9 Cross US 421.
The road ahead is called Old Bedford–Milton Pike. It's one of those one-and-a-half-lane paved roads that are always a pleasure to ride.

11.8 Start a descent.
Watch for loose gravel. As it drops from the ridgetop, the road enters a thickly wooded hollow and passes a waterfall.

14.4 Straight as Old Bedford–Milton Pike joins US 421.

14.7 Pass the Our House restaurant.

15.8 Start a big descent into the Ohio Valley.
This is where you lose the elevation you painstakingly gained at mile 2.2. A sign warns truckers: USE LOWER GEAR.

The road bends sharply left at the bottom of the hill, where a runaway truck ramp awaits. Presumably, it works for runaway bikes, too, but I'd hate to put it to the test.

17.1 Left as you enter Milton. Stay on US 421.
Milton has several stores and a restaurant.

17.1 Cross the Ohio River on a big steel cantilever bridge.
This is not an easy bridge to cross. It has two narrow lanes and no walkway. On top of that, it has two finger joints that can swallow skinny bike tires. The best approach is to wait for a gap in the traffic flow and then take the lane, slowing to a crawl as you cross the finger joints. Traffic may back up behind you, but resist the urge to squeeze over. Most drivers realize what you are up against. You'll be across soon enough, and the cars can pass you then.

Someday this bridge may be much easier to cross. There is talk about building a new bridge and keeping this one for walkers and cyclists. But that would be a long way off, if it happens at all.

17.9 Enter Indiana.
The President Madison Inn is off to your right.

18.0 Left on Second Street at the T-junction.

18.1 Right on Baltimore Street.

18.2 Left on Main Street. Downtown Madison is ahead.
Madison is the perfect Ohio River port, and its well-kept appearance is a reproach

to the many other towns along the river that have grown shabby. The downtown business district looks prosperous, the old houses are in good order, and the river-front is accessible. The Ohio Theatre still shows first-run movies.

18.4 Left on Jefferson Street, at the Jefferson County Courthouse.

18.7 Right on Vaughn Drive.
If you were to go any farther down Jefferson Street you'd be on the boat ramp. One of the proposals for a new Ohio River bridge puts it right here.

Vaughn Drive runs parallel to the river. A walkway, with benches and wide spots that overlook the river, runs alongside the street. From the walkway you can see the riverbank and boat landing below. In the summer this stretch of the Ohio is packed with pleasure boats each weekend. Every July a speedboat race called the Madison Regatta is held here. Some of those boats can hit 150 miles per hour.

19.2 Right on Vine Street, at the Lanier Mansion.
The house is a state historic site and is open for public tours.

19.4 Right on Main Street.
The main downtown business district runs between here and the courthouse. You can find a wide range of restaurants in the immediate area, from lunch counters to the kind with white tablecloths. Look left to see the fountain as you cross Broadway.

20.2 Right on Baltimore Street.

20.3 Left on Second Street.

20.4 Right onto the bridge approach road.
It's time to face that bridge again. You rode it once, so you know you can do it again. You reenter Kentucky almost as soon as you start across the bridge. Kentucky used to be part of Virginia, and Virginia's land claim extended to the far side of the Ohio River.

21.2 Curve left as you leave the bridge, and then make a hard right on KY 36 at the T-junction.
KY 421, and most of the traffic, turns right and heads up the hill, but our route goes left to follow the river.

21.3 Right at a blinking yellow light.
From here the road follows the Ohio River all the way back to Carrollton. The river

remains in view much of the way, and you have good views of the bluffs on the Indiana side.

31.7 Straight as US 42 joins from the left.

32.8 Straight as KY 55 joins from the left.
Now you can see the Carrollton Bridge.

33.1 Cross the Kentucky River and enter Carrollton.

33.2 Left on Second Street.

33.3 End the ride at Point Park.

Bicycle Shops

None near the route.

Lodging

The Carrollton Inn (502-732-6905), built in 1805, is on Main Street in Carrollton, just one block east of the starting point. In Madison you can stay at the President Madison Motel (812-265-2361), which is located near the bridge at mile 17.9 on the route. Camping is available at General Butler State Park near Carrollton and at Clifty Falls State Park near Madison.

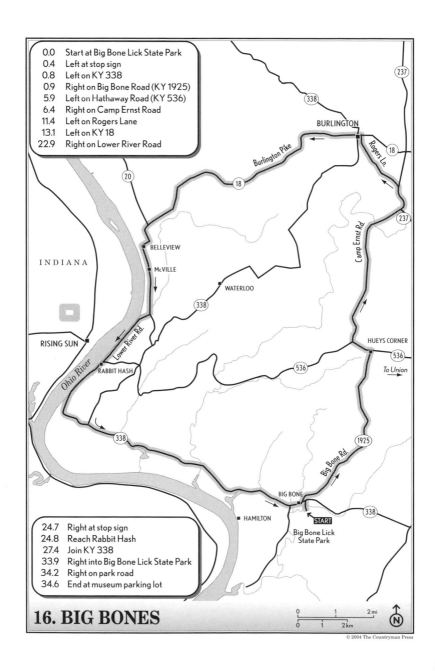

0.0	Start at Big Bone Lick State Park
0.4	Left at stop sign
0.8	Left on KY 338
0.9	Right on Big Bone Road (KY 1925)
5.9	Left on Hathaway Road (KY 536)
6.4	Right on Camp Ernst Road
11.4	Left on Rogers Lane
13.1	Left on KY 18
22.9	Right on Lower River Road

24.7	Right at stop sign
24.8	Reach Rabbit Hash
27.4	Join KY 338
33.9	Right into Big Bone Lick State Park
34.2	Right on park road
34.6	End at museum parking lot

16. BIG BONES

Big Bones

- **DISTANCE:** 34.6 miles
- **HIGHLIGHTS:** Big Bone Lick, rich bottomland along the Ohio River, and the most photographed country store in the state

During the last ice age, from 20,000 to 12,000 years ago, Big Bone Lick was a salty mudhole visited by large mammals, including mammoths, mastodons, musk oxen, and horses. They came for the salt, but some died in the mud, which preserved their bones.

French explorers arrived in 1739 to find the ground littered with big bones, some of which they shipped back to France. Meriwether Lewis—half of the Lewis and Clark duo—visited in 1803 on his way to join the famous expedition. William Clark collected bones here for Thomas Jefferson in 1807, after their long journey to the Pacific was over.

Today the mud has almost dried up, and all the good fossils have been shipped out. All that's left is a nice little state park with a modest museum.

Though almost completely rural, this tour lies close to Cincinnati and passes within a few miles of some highly built-up areas. If you are driving out from Cincinnati or its suburbs, you may find it convenient to start at Central Park and Arboretum on Camp Ernst Road (mile 7.6).

Cincinnati motorcyclists like to congregate at the Rabbit Hash country store (mile 24.8). On any nice weekend day, you should expect to see lots of them on the roads in and out of Rabbit Hash. But motorcyclists are always generous about sharing the road, so you won't have any problem with them. Now, if it were coal trucks congregating at the country store, you'd have something to worry about.

DIRECTIONS FOR THE RIDE

0.0 Start at the museum parking lot in Big Bone Lick State Park.
A short trail (foot traffic only) leads to what is left of the lick. The museum exhibits some of the big bones and tells their story. Only one road leads out.

0.4 Left at the stop sign.
A right turn here would take you up a steep hill to the park campground.

0.8 Left on KY 338.

0.9 Right on Big Bone Road (KY 1925) and start climbing.
If you aren't quite awake yet, this steep grade will get the juices flowing.

5.9 Left on Hathaway Road (KY 536) at a T-junction.
The community here is called Hueys Corner. There are no services.

6.4 Right on Camp Ernst Road.

7.6 Pass Central Park and Arboretum on the right.
This is a big municipal park with picnic tables, year-round toilets, and water. The local cycling club starts some rides here.

11.4 Left on Rogers Lane at the traffic light.
There is a small store here.

13.1 Left on KY 18 in downtown Burlington.
This is the Boone County seat, with big government buildings but little in the way of stores and restaurants. Most of the commercial development is to the east of the tour.

16.5 Pass Vice Lane on the right.
As far as I can tell, it fails to live up to its name. But you never know.

18.0 Start a mile-long descent into the Ohio Valley.
The drop from the Bluegrass Plateau to Ohio bottomland almost always makes for

a good ride, and this one does not disappoint. The road is smooth and lined with trees on both sides.

19.3 Pass Middle Creek Road on the left.
A side trip down this road can take you to Boone County Cliffs State Nature Preserve, with hiking trails and cliffside views. The detour adds 3.4 miles of biking, plus a mile or so of walking if you want to see the cliffs.

19.5 Pass Dinsmore Homestead on the right.
James Dinsmore bought the land in 1838 and the place stayed in his family's hands till 1988, when a nonprofit organization took over. Public tours are available, but the schedule is very limited.

Just past the Dinsmore Homestead, and also on the right, you find the entrance to Dinsmore Woods State Nature Preserve.

19.9 Reach flat bottomland near the Ohio River.

20.7 Enter Belleview.
The small grocery on the right bears a sign for THE STORE.

Ohio River bottomland.

22.9 Right on Lower River Road.

The sign says ROAD CLOSED but don't believe it. Bikes can still get through.

Cyclists need to read between the lines on road signs. A ROAD ENDS sign usually means exactly what it says. The road ends at a steep hill or a creek or an interstate, and you'll have to turn around. In contrast, a ROAD CLOSED sign often means the road actually goes through but has been closed to motor traffic because money wasn't available to repair an unsafe bridge or washed-out roadway. Cyclists can usually sneak past such closures. Then again, sometimes ROAD CLOSED means the bridge was swept away in a flood 10 years ago, and you're out of luck. That's what keeps it interesting.

23.3 Dismount and walk around the concrete barrier.

You can now see why the road was closed to motor traffic. It runs along a steep riverbank where erosion is taking its toll.

23.5 Dismount again and walk around the second barrier. You have now left the closed part of the road.

Lower River Road is well named. All too often, maps lie when they show roads running right next to rivers. You think you'll be riding the riverbank, but when you get there the water is nowhere in sight. That's not a problem here, though. If you were any closer to the Ohio River, you'd need to swim.

Rising Sun, Indiana, is just across the river. These days the town is known mainly for its huge riverboat, which dominates the shoreline. It's not a real riverboat. It's just a floating casino built to satisfy the Indiana law that allows gambling only on watercraft.

24.7 Right at the stop sign. A small wooden sign points to Rabbit Hash.

24.8 Reach Rabbit Hash, site of a famous and much-photographed country store.

Country stores once supplied rural residents with almost everything they needed but could not make at home. The automobile killed that kind of store decades ago, though it hung on longer in Kentucky than in most other states. Today country people drive to town where they shop in big stores like everyone else.

Country stores still exist, however, and they come in three varieties. The best stores are closely tied to the local population. The owners know their customers, who often seem to use the store as much for social contact as for merchandise. The second category consists of big-company convenience stores, often bearing the name of an oil company. They look almost exactly like their city counterparts. No one gets excited about such stores, but they meet your needs when you are hungry or thirsty.

The last category is made up of tourist stores. They look cuter than any real country store ever did, and they stock more souvenirs than sundries. The Rabbit Hash store definitely falls into this category, but at least it's not a modern fake. It really was a country store, dating from 1831.

27.4 Join KY 338 and continue straight.

30.6 Cross Gunpowder Creek, a navigable stream with boat docks.

30.7 Reach Union.
Union has a store, a marina, and a commercial campground called Camp Turnabout. The next mile offers good views of Ohio River bottomland to the right.

33.9 Right into Big Bone Lick Park

34.2 Right on the park road. A sign points to the museum.

34.6 End the ride at the museum parking lot.

Bicycle Shops

Montgomery Cyclery, 3708 Dixie Highway, Erlanger; 859-342-7300

Reser Outfitters, 735 Monmouth Street, Newport; 859-261-6187

Lodging

There are no motels or hotels on the route. A Days Inn (859-485-4151) and an Econolodge (859-485-4123) are located 7.6 miles east of the park, where KY 338 meets I-71 and I-75. Big Bone Lick State Park has a fine campground with a small store, but you have to climb a very steep hill to get there. You'll find commercial campgrounds at miles 23.3 and 30.7.

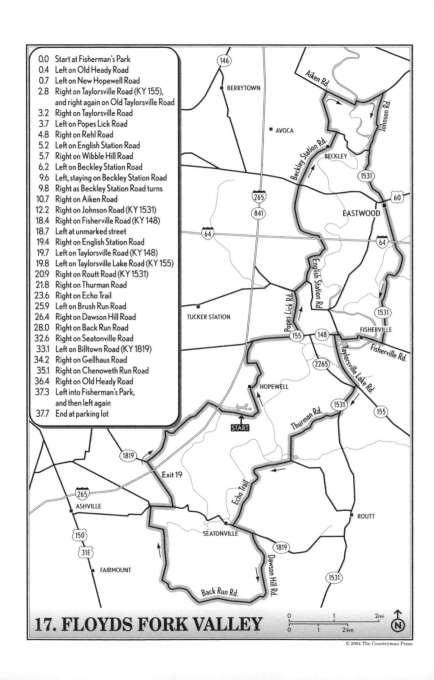

0.0	Start at Fisherman's Park
0.4	Left on Old Heady Road
0.7	Left on New Hopewell Road
2.8	Right on Taylorsville Road (KY 155), and right again on Old Taylorsville Road
3.2	Right on Taylorsville Road
3.7	Left on Popes Lick Road
4.8	Right on Rehl Road
5.2	Left on English Station Road
5.7	Right on Wibble Hill Road
6.2	Left on Beckley Station Road
9.6	Left, staying on Beckley Station Road
9.8	Right as Beckley Station Road turns
10.7	Right on Aiken Road
12.2	Right on Johnson Road (KY 1531)
18.4	Right on Fisherville Road (KY 148)
18.7	Left at unmarked street
19.4	Right on English Station Road
19.7	Left on Taylorsville Road (KY 148)
19.8	Left on Taylorsville Lake Road (KY 155)
20.9	Right on Routt Road (KY 1531)
21.8	Right on Thurman Road
23.6	Right on Echo Trail
25.9	Left on Brush Run Road
26.4	Right on Dawson Hill Road
28.0	Right on Back Run Road
32.6	Right on Seatonville Road
33.1	Left on Billtown Road (KY 1819)
34.2	Right on Gellhaus Road
35.1	Right on Chenoweth Run Road
36.4	Right on Old Heady Road
37.3	Left into Fisherman's Park, and then left again
37.7	End at parking lot

17. FLOYDS FORK VALLEY

0   1   2mi
0   1   2 km

N

Floyds Fork Valley

- **DISTANCE:** 37.7 miles
- **HIGHLIGHTS:** Scenic valley views and classic bridges

Almost every kind of landscape has its fans. Some people favor the high mountains, while others prefer the seashore. For my money, it's hard to beat a compact, enclosed valley full of well-watered, fertile farms. Such a place always reminds me of Woody Guthrie's "This Land Is Your Land"—not the part everybody knows, but the seldom-sung second verse in which he sings about the "golden valley." For me, the golden valley has always been a place where life is good, the weather is always fine, and the cares of the outside world never penetrate. Whenever you go there, it feels like home. The Bluegrass has several golden valleys, and I can never decide which is best. But Floyds Fork is a good one. (For two other examples, check out the Salt River west of Lawrenceburg on tours 5 and 24 and the lower Kentucky River on tour 20.)

The survival of this bucolic enclave is surprising, since it lies within Kentucky's most populous county, Jefferson. A tributary of the Salt River, Floyds Fork flows north to south just east of Louisville. Technically, this ride remains within the Louisville city limits, now that Louisville and Jefferson County have formed a joint city-county government. But there is nothing urban about it. A small part of the ride goes through ritzy suburbs, but otherwise it's nothing but farms, forest, and a few villages.

This ride has more elevation gain per mile than most Bluegrass rides. A road along the riverbank would make for easy riding, but no such road exists. The roads here go up and down between the valley floor and the bluffs. The scenery is good, but the riding can be hard.

The route follows a pinched loop with a narrow waist. You can easily turn it into two shorter rides by cutting across the waist on Taylorsville Road, between miles 3.7 and 19.8.

It's possible to reach this tour by Louisville city bus. Take the Number 61 bus out Shelbyville Road. Get off where the bus turns left on Beckley Heights Drive. Continue east on Shelbyville Road by bike till you reach Beckley Station Road. Turn left there and you are at mile 8.0 on the tour. If you plan to take the bus, call 502-585-1234 a day ahead and ask that they send a bus fitted with a bike rack. This works fine on the way out, but can be tricky on the trip home because it's difficult to put an exact time on when you'll finish.

DIRECTIONS FOR THE RIDE

Start at Fisherman's Park on Old Heady Road just east of I-265. To get there by car, take I-265 to Exit 23 and go east on Taylorsville Road. Take the first right and go 2.4 miles. The park entrance will be on the right. Turn left on entering the park and follow the park road to its end, where a gravel parking lot overlooks three small lakes.

0.0 Leave the parking lot on a dirt road, which soon turns to rough asphalt.

0.4 Left on Old Heady Road.

0.7 Left at unmarked fork to New Hopewell Road.
At mile 1.0 look through the trees to the right for a glimpse of the Floyds Fork Valley.

2.8 Right on Taylorsville Road (KY 155). Turn right again almost immediately on Old Taylorsville Road (unmarked).
Look right for a small waterfall.

3.2 Right on Taylorsville Road as the old road rejoins the main one.
Expect heavy traffic for the next half mile.

3.7 Left on Popes Lick Road and pass under an old railroad bridge.
This is a mighty big bridge for a rather small creek, but railroads can't dip down into the valley the way roads do.

4.8 Right on Rehl Road.

5.2 Left on English Station Road.

5.7 Right on Wibble Hill Road.

6.2 Left on Beckley Station Road.

6.4 Pass through a short tunnel under I-64.
For the next 2 miles the road goes through a suburb.

8.0 Cross US 60 at a traffic light.
This is the center of Beckley. The business district includes a convenience store and a couple of restaurants. You can reach this spot by Louisville city bus.

9.2 Cross railroad tracks.

9.6 Left at a T-junction. Beckley Station Road continues to the left, but the sign doesn't make that clear.

9.8 Right as Beckley Station Road makes a 90-degree turn.

10.7 Right on Aiken Road.
This road was recently closed for bridge replacement, but cyclists can still get through for the time being.

11.5 Cross Floyds Fork.
Though the route has stayed within or close to the Floyds Fork Valley so far, this is the first spot that offers a good view of the actual stream. Take a look at the old bridge on the left—if it's still standing.

12.2 Right on Johnson Road (KY 1531).
Keep an eye out for good views on the right.

14.2 Cross railroad tracks.
The crossing is rough and slanted.

14.9 Cross US 60 and enter Eastwood village.

15.0 Cross Eastwood Cutoff.

Figaro's Pizzeria and Restaurant occupies the northeast corner. Pancakes and pizza (not necessarily at the same time) are two traditional cycling fuels. I don't know where, or even if, you can find good pancakes in the Floyds Fork Valley, but this is the place for pizza.

15.8 Cross I-64 in a short tunnel.
The creek just ahead is Long Run, a major tributary of Floyds Fork.

18.3 Cross under railroad tracks.

18.4 Right on Fisherville Road (KY 148) at the T-junction.

18.6 Cross Floyds Fork.
Look for the old railroad bridge on the right.

18.7 Left at an unmarked street. A sign points to the Fisherville Post Office. Go one block, and then turn right on Old Fisherville Road.
You are now on the old highway, which runs through the heart of Fisherville.

19.4 Right on English Station Road.

The golden valley.

19.7 Left on Taylorsville Road (KY 148).
A grocery store occupies the southeast corner.

19.8 Left on Taylorsville Lake Road (KY 155).

19.9 Cross Floyds Fork yet again and start a mile-long climb.
This is a busy road, but it has a wide, paved shoulder—the only one on the tour.
Watch out for the rumble strips, though. They'll shake your wheels off.

20.9 Right on Routt Road (KY 1531).

21.8 Right on Thurman Road.

23.6 Right on Echo Trail.

25.9 Left on Brush Run Road.

26.4 Right on Dawson Hill Road.
When you see a road named for a hill, you can usually expect a climb, so pick a low
gear and get started. For most of the way, the road parallels a tiny creek with a
rocky bed.

28.0 Right on Back Run Road, which runs into Broad Run Road.

30.4 Cross Floyds Fork for the last time.
After crossing some dead-flat bottomland, start the last big climb as the road
leaves the Floyds Fork Valley for good.

32.6 Right on Seatonville Road at a T-junction.

33.1 Left on Billtown Road (KY 1819).

33.8 Cross I-265.

34.2 Right on Gellhaus Road.

35.1 Right on Chenoweth Run Road at a T-junction.

36.4 Right on Old Heady Road (unmarked) at a T-junction.

36.7 Cross I-265.

37.3 Left into Fisherman's Park, and then left again inside the park.

37.7 End at the parking lot.

Bicycle Shops

Adrenaline Zone, 614 East Washington Street, Louisville; 502-595-6655

Bardstown Road Bicycles, 1051 Bardstown Road, Louisville; 502-485-9795

Bicycle Sport, 128 Breckenridge Lane, Louisville; 502-897-2611

City BMX, 743 East Washington Street, Louisville; 502-561-0269

Dixie Schwinn, 1803 Rockford Lane, Louisville (in the Shively suburb); 502-448-3448

Highland Cycle, 1737 Bardstown Road, Louisville; 502-458-7832

St. Matthews Schwinn, 106 Sears Avenue, Louisville; 502-895-0553

Scheller's, 11520 Shelbyville Road, Louisville (in the Middletown suburb); 502-245-1955

Scheller's, 8323 Preston Highway, Louisville (in the Okolona suburb); 502-969-4100

Lodging

None along the route, but nearby Louisville offers rooms in just about every price range, unless you are foolish enough to visit during Derby week.

18

Pilot Knob

- **DISTANCE:** 41.1 miles (44.6 miles including alternate route), plus an optional 2.2 miles of hiking
- **HIGHLIGHTS:** Pilot Knob, Winchester, the Eskippakithiki Indian village, and Lulbegrud Creek

The high point of this tour, both literally and figuratively, is the bare-rock summit of Pilot Knob. This is the spot from which Daniel Boone first beheld the Bluegrass. It still offers a superb view—some say the best in Kentucky.

Including this ride in the book required bending the rules a little. For one thing, Pilot Knob is not quite in the Bluegrass. As the name suggests, it lies in the Knobs, a narrow band of hills that wraps around the Bluegrass on all sides but the north. For another thing, you can't finish this tour on your bike. You must walk the last 2.2 miles, though it's well worth it.

A big part of Pilot Knob's appeal lies in its obscurity. It is well off the beaten path. In some states, a place with the historic importance and natural beauty of Pilot Knob would be highly developed, with a visitors center, huge parking lot, plenty of signs, and maybe even an admission charge. But the Kentucky authorities almost ignore it. It's not even a state park, just a lowly nature preserve. Only one sign marks its location, and it's easy to miss. Once you get there you'll find almost no facilities—no rest rooms, no explanatory sign, no picnic tables, and no drinking water unless you trust the spring half a mile up the trail. All I can say about that neglect is: Thanks, Kentucky! Pilot Knob is great just the way it is.

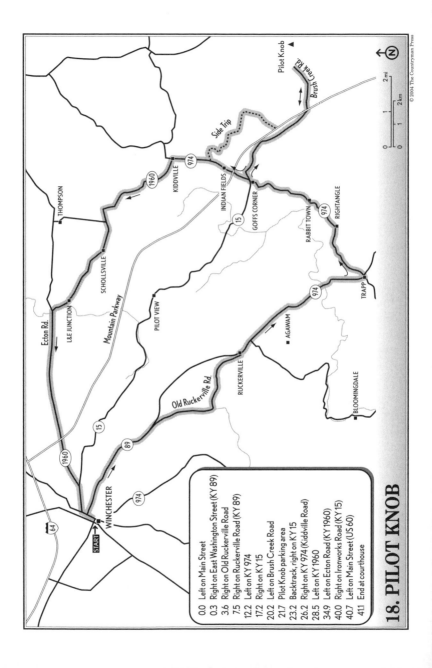

18. PILOT KNOB

0.0	Left on Main Street
0.3	Right on East Washington Street (KY 89)
3.6	Right on Old Ruckerville Road
7.5	Right on Ruckerville Road (KY 89)
12.2	Left on KY 974
17.2	Right on KY 15
20.2	Left on Brush Creek Road
21.7	Pilot Knob parking area
23.2	Backtrack, right on KY 15
26.2	Right on KY 974 (Kiddville Road)
28.5	Left on KY 1960
34.9	Left on Ecton Road (KY 1960)
40.0	Right on Ironworks Road (KY 15)
40.7	Left on Main Street (US 60)
41.1	End at courthouse

© 2004 The Countryman Press

Since this trip requires some walking, make sure you have the shoes for it. The trail is steep and can be muddy. If you ride in cleated bike shoes, you should pack hiking boots, or at least sneakers.

One small warning: This route, especially the first half, has more than its share of bike-chasing dogs. Whatever your technique for dealing with dogs, be ready to use it.

By the way, it's possible that Boone never really visited Pilot Knob. He may have climbed some other hill. But Kentuckians never let facts get in the way of a good Daniel Boone story, and neither should you.

Winchester, where the ride begins, still has an active downtown business district, though the big stores are all out on the bypass now. You can find several restaurants and a grocery store within a few blocks of the courthouse. If you need supplies, stock up here. You'll find nothing bigger than a country store for the next 40 miles.

DIRECTIONS FOR THE RIDE

Start in front of the Clark County Courthouse on Main Street in downtown Winchester. Even on weekdays you can find a parking spot within a block or two.

0.0 Left on Main Street as you leave the courthouse.

0.3 Right on East Washington Street, also known as KY 89.

1.3 Stay on KY 89 as you leave the built-up part of Winchester.

3.6 Right on Old Ruckerville Road.

4.9 Pass under a tall railroad bridge.

5.4 Cross the railroad again, this time in a short, narrow tunnel.
The next half mile gives you the first steep climb of the day.

6.7 Reach a ridge with good views right and left.
On a clear day you can see the Cumberland Mountains on the left—proof that the Bluegrass plain does not go on forever.

7.5 Right on Ruckerville Road (KY 89).
You immediately cross Dry Fork Creek. There is a small waterfall just upstream.

8.4 Start a long, gentle downhill run.
The landscape here has a big-sky, western look not often found in Kentucky. I think it's the lack of trees close to the road, coupled with the view of distant mountains.

12.2 Left on KY 974, in the village of Trapp.
Fox's General Store is on your left as you make the turn. The business dates from 1900, but the current building is much newer. Like many country stores in Kentucky, Fox's includes a restaurant of sorts where you can buy a hot meal.

The road from here to KY 15 is a cyclist's dream, with short, steep hills and lots of curves.

17.2 Right on KY 15 at Goffs Corner.
You have a rare treat here: not one, but two country stores at the same intersection.

18.5 Cross Lulbegrud Creek and enter Powell County.
Just short of the bridge a path branches left down to the creek. Locals come here to swim and fish.

Daniel Boone and his party camped here, or nearby, in the winter of 1769–70. They named the creek, and it's quite a story. (Unlike most Boone stories, this one is true. I think.) The men had a copy of Gulliver's Travels, *and read it by their campfire. One day, on returning to camp, a man announced that he had been to Lorbrulgrud and killed two residents there. In Jonathan Swift's book, Lorbrulgrud was the capital of Brobdingnag. The man had actually been upstream at the oil springs, and the residents he killed were buffalo. The name stuck, though the spelling has changed.*

19.4 Enter the village of West Bend (no services).

20.2 Left on Brush Creek Road.
The Pilot Knob historical sign stands at the southeast corner. Small and easy to miss, this sign is the only official clue to the location and significance of Pilot Knob. Few motorized travelers would even notice it. And if they are traveling on the adjacent Mountain Parkway, as most do, they see no sign at all.

21.7 Stop at the parking area, where the pavement ends. Visitors who arrive by car walk from here, but you can bike 500 feet farther on a dirt road.
There are two schools of thought on parking bicycles at trailheads. Some people

A view of the Bluegrass from Pilot Knob.

hide their bikes in the woods. Others think it safer to lock bikes up in plain sight. If you're in the first camp, you'll probably want to ride to the end of the dirt road. If you're in the second, you should leave your bike at the paved parking area. I've done it both ways and never had any trouble.

The following directions cover the walk up Pilot Knob. Allow about two hours for the hike, including a generous rest at the top to take in the view. You could probably do it in an hour, but why rush?

Pilot Knob Hike

0.0 Take the dirt road out of the paved parking area.

0.1 Ford Brush Creek where the dirt road ends.
Most days you can do this without wetting your feet. Climb the steps and pass through the narrow gate meant to deter motor vehicles. The real trail starts here.

0.2 Keep left at the fork.
The trail on the right leads to an old millstone quarry. Save it for the return trip, if you have the time and energy to spare.

0.7 Pass a spring.

1.1 Reach the top, known as Boone's Overlook. Watch out for poison ivy in the last, steep stretch.
Some details have changed since Boone's day (the four-lane Mountain Parkway, for one), but the view remains spectacular. The overlook faces northwest. Ahead, the Bluegrass stretches out toward Winchester and Lexington. Other knobs rise beside each flank of the one you're standing on, topping out at about the same elevation. To the left, behind the knobs, is the unbroken wall of the Cumberland Mountains.
    When you are ready to leave, retrace your steps to the trailhead.

2.0 Reach the turnoff for the Millstone Quarry Trail.
If you're up for more walking, take this side trail to a long-abandoned quarry where millstones were cut from the conglomerate rock. It adds just under a mile to your trip.
    Bike mileage resumes below.

21.7 Leave the trailhead parking area and go west on Brush Creek Road.

23.2 Right on KY 15.

26.2 Right on KY 974 (Kiddville Road) at Goffs Corner.
The farm behind the church raises alpacas.

27.0 Reach Indian Fields. A few houses are clustered here, but no sign identifies the spot.
This community has a long history, and its name has changed several times. It used to be called Indian Old Fields. Before that it was Indian Old Corn Fields, and before that, Eskippakithiki. Shawnee Indians gave it the last name, which means "Place of Blue Licks." The blue licks were oily salt springs, which attracted game. The Shawnees lived and farmed here during the first half of the 18th century. They abandoned it in 1754, several years before Anglo-American settlers began to move in.
    Some history books claim that Eskippakithiki was Kentucky's only Indian settlement in historic times. That seems unlikely, but no one can point with certainty to any others. In any case, few if any Native Americans lived in the Bluegrass when Boone and his comrades arrived. Indians visited the region, and they traveled through it on the Warriors' Path and other routes, but they didn't settle down— except in Eskippakithiki, for a few decades.
    At its peak, Eskippakithiki covered about 3,500 acres. It included a fort, at the

center of which stood a pole where criminals were put to death. Cabins were scattered over the open plain, which supported crops of corn, tobacco, and beans. But by the time Boone arrived in 1769, the Indians were gone and the fort had been burned.

27.4 Pass Oil Springs Road on the right. The main tour goes straight.
A side trip to the right adds 3.5 miles to the tour by way of the oil springs. After the asphalt turns to gravel, look for a small stream crossing the road. You can see an oil slick on the water. Today we regard oil as a pollutant and try to keep it out of our streams, but a century ago people (some people, anyway) regarded the oily water as healthful. A spa was built here, but no trace of it remains.

28.5 Left on KY 1960.

33.7 Pass the ruins of a railroad bridge over Georges Branch.

34.9 Left on Ecton Road. You are still on KY 1960.
The landscape shifts from rural to suburban as you approach Winchester. Farms give way to new houses on acre lots.

38.6 Cross over Mountain Parkway.

40.0 Right on Ironworks Road.
This is KY 15, though no sign at the intersection tells you so. There's a convenience store at the corner, but you probably won't need it. The trip is almost over.

40.2 Enter Winchester.

40.7 Left on Main Street, also known as US 60.

41.1 End at the courthouse.

Bicycle Shops

The closest are in Lexington, some 20 miles west of the starting point.

Lodging

There is a Best Western (859-744-7210) on Lexington Avenue (US 60), 1.9 miles west of the starting point. You can find a wider range of choices at Exit 94 off I-64, about 20 miles northwest of downtown Winchester. The closest campground is at Fort Boonesborough State Park, about 10 miles southwest of Winchester.

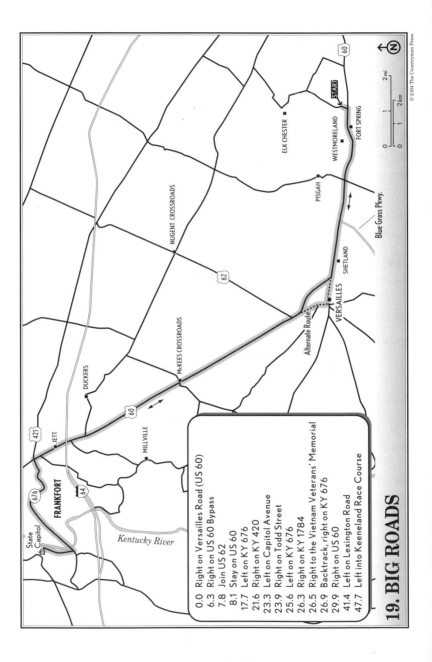

19. BIG ROADS

0.0 Right on Versailles Road (US 60)
6.3 Right on US 60 Bypass
7.8 Join US 62
8.1 Stay on US 60
17.7 Left on KY 676
21.6 Right on KY 420
23.3 Left on Capitol Avenue
23.9 Right on Todd Street
25.6 Left on KY 676
26.3 Right on KY 1784
26.5 Right to the Vietnam Veterans' Memorial
26.9 Backtrack, right on KY 676
29.9 Right on US 60
41.4 Left on Lexington Road
47.7 Left into Keeneland Race Course

State Capitol

FRANKFORT

Kentucky River

JETT

DUCKERS

MILLVILLE

McKEES CROSSROADS

NUGENT CROSSROADS

Alternate Route

VERSAILLES

SHETLAND

Blue Grass Pkwy.

PISGAH

ELK CHESTER

WESTMORELAND

FORT SPRING

START

© 2004 The Countryman Press

19

Big Roads

■ **DISTANCE:** 47.7 miles

■ **HIGHLIGHTS:** The Capitol, the Kentucky's Vietnam Veterans' Memorial, Keeneland Race Course, and some of the finest horse farms in the Bluegrass

This tour connects Lexington, the cultural capital of the Bluegrass, with Frankfort, the political capital of Kentucky. Unique among the tours described here, it follows main highways. Some cyclists will hate this tour because the roads are wide and see substantial traffic, including trucks. Others may like it because it provides a wide, paved shoulder almost all the way. If you hate to share lanes with motor vehicles, or if you like to ride two abreast mile after mile, this tour is for you.

This is an out-and-back ride, not a loop, so you won't miss much if you turn it into a one-way trip. Or you might consider taking this tour on the way out and returning by another route, such as Old Frankfort Pike. Mileage starts at the Lexington end, but if you live closer to Frankfort you might as well start there.

DIRECTIONS FOR THE RIDE

Start at Keeneland Race Course on US 60 west of Lexington. Parking won't be a problem unless it's a race day. (For more on Keeneland, see Ride 7.)

0.0 Right on Versailles Road (US 60) as you leave the Keeneland parking lot. *The road before you is typical of what you'll be riding on almost the whole trip. It's a*

four-lane divided highway with wide, paved shoulders. The shoulder isn't marked as a bike lane, but it beats many that are. It's smooth—well, reasonably smooth—and it gets almost no cross traffic.

2.2 Cross Parkers Mill Road (KY 1968).
The Keenelodge Motor Inn is on the left, with a small grocery next door.

2.6 Enter Woodford County.
This is the second of three counties you will ride in today. The other two are Fayette, where you started, and Franklin, which lies ahead.

2.9 Pass a castle.
Castles are not common sights in Kentucky. This one dates from 1969. It was built as a private house—albeit a rather big one with six bedrooms and over 10,000 square feet of living space—but the owner never moved in. The place was on the market for many years, with an ordinary FOR SALE sign hanging on the fence.

Just beyond the castle is the Castle Hill Farm, which includes a winery open to the public.

Frankfort welcomes visitors with a model of the new Capitol building.

3.6 Pass a crossroads with three convenience stores and a doughnut shop.

4.4 Cross the Blue Grass Parkway.
Watch out for traffic at the exit ramp.

4.9 Pass Crittenden Cabin, set back from the road on the right.
Major John Crittenden, a Revolutionary War veteran, built the cabin in 1783.

6.3 Right on US 60 Bypass.
You are now in the midst of Versailles's main business district. Within a few hundred yards you can find two supermarkets and several restaurants. The McDonald's on the right has a hydrant on its front lawn—perfect for filling water bottles.

If you prefer to ride through town, go straight instead of right to take the US 60 Business Route. Rejoin the main route at mile 7.8.

7.6 Pass under a pedestrian bridge.
If you take the next left you will find a convenience store and a Dairy Queen within two blocks. Those are your last sources of food and drink for 10 miles.

7.8 Join US 62, which comes in from the left.
If you took the US 60 Business Route, you rejoin the main tour here.

8.1 Stay on US 60 as US 68 splits right.

13.7 Pass a vineyard.
A few years ago you would have had to look hard for a row of grapevines in the Bluegrass. A few people grew grapes in their backyards, but there was no commercial production. That's now changing, and young vineyards like the one on your right have appeared in several Bluegrass counties.

15.8 Enter Franklin County.

16.5 Pass under I-64 and enter the village of Jett, now part of greater Frankfort.
Two big hotels, a Best Western and a Fairfield Inn, stand near the freeway exit.

17.7 Left on KY 676.
A modest motel, the Bluegrass Inn, occupies the northwest corner.

21.6 Right on KY 420.
The tour follows two-lane roads for the next few miles. If you really want to avoid them, turn around here. But then you'll miss the Capitol.

22.7 Pass under the Capitol Garage.
You are now almost directly under the Capitol, but you can't see it from here.

23.1 Pass the Little Market, an old-fashioned corner store.

23.3 Left on Capitol Avenue. You can't miss the Capitol now. Follow the street as it loops around the Capitol building.
The Capitol opened in 1910, but some Kentuckians still call it the New Capitol to distinguish it from its predecessor, the Old Capitol, which still stands in downtown Frankfort. Like most state capitols, it is an imposing sight—over 400 feet long, with an exterior of granite and Bedford limestone. The interior may be even more impressive, with granite columns, marble floors, and statues of famous Kentuckians.

The turnaround point for this tour is behind the Capitol, near the floral clock. When you're ready to start back, go to the front of the Capitol and head down Capitol Avenue.

23.9 Right on Todd Street.

25.6 Left on KY 676.

26.3 Right on KY 1784. A sign points to the Vietnam Veterans' Memorial.

26.5 Right to the Vietnam Veterans' Memorial, which is not well marked. The sign says KENTUCKY DEPARTMENT FOR LIBRARIES.
The memorial is a gem, quite possibly the best war memorial I've seen anywhere. It consists of a giant sundial. The sundial's base is a stone pavement bearing the names of all the Kentuckians who died in the Vietnam War. The gnomon—the part of the sundial that sticks up—casts its shadow on the names. On the anniversary of each person's death, the tip of the shadow grazes the carved name. But that's not all. The names are arranged by years so that as the day passes, the shadow touches each year in turn. Follow it around and you can see how just a few Kentuckians fell in the war's early and final years. But the names mount up in the late 1960s.

Leave the way you came, back toward KY 676.

26.9 Right on KY 676.

29.9 Right on US 60.

31.2 Pass under I-64.

31.9 Enter Woodford County.

32.6 Pass a trailer park.
Look right for two businesses that seem out of place on the open road: Rebecca Ruth Bourbon Candy and the Paul Sawyier Art Gallery. Bourbon candy is a local tradition. I prefer my bourbon and candy unmixed, but you'll have to decide for yourself. If you've never tried it, here's your chance.

Paul Sawyier's art is also a local tradition. Sawyier (1865–1917) is probably the best-known Kentucky painter. (Best known, not best. The best is Harlan Hubbard.) He spent much of his working life in and near Frankfort, living for a while in a Kentucky River houseboat that served as home and studio. Sawyier prints hang on many a Bluegrass wall, and you can buy them here.

39.9 Curve left as US 60 (your route) splits from US 62 and US 60 Business.

11.1 Left on Lexington Road.
A walk-bike path begins at mile 41.7. It runs on the right side of the highway for almost a mile before turning into the Methodist Camp. It's not a bad ride, but the highway shoulder is just as good.

43.4 Cross under the Blue Grass Parkway.

43.9 Pass a doughnut shop and convenience stores.

45.2 Enter Fayette County.

45.9 Cross Old Versailles Road.
If you're growing tired of the big road, turn right here for a short detour through Fort Spring, one of Fayette County's old African American villages. Its name has changed several times. According to one story, the community goes back to 1826, when three freed slaves settled here and named their home Reform. Slaves from nearby farms came here for nighttime meetings, and that practice led to the name Slipaway, which became Slickaway. In 1886 patrons of the Slickaway Post Office (now closed) asked for what they considered a more dignified name, Fort Spring.

47.7 Left into Keeneland Race Course to end at the parking lot.

Bicycle Shops

Dodds Cyclery, 1985 Harrodsburg Road, Lexington; 859-277-6013

Pedal Power, 401 South Upper Street, Lexington; 859-255-6408

Scheller's, 212 Woodland Avenue, Lexington; 859-233-1764

Vicious Cycle, Todds Road at Codell, Lexington; 859-263-7300

Lodging

Lexington and Frankfort both offer a wide range of motels and hotels. Some are right on the route: the Keenelodge Motor Inn (859-254-6699) at mile 2.2, the Best Western (502-695-6111) and Fairfield Inn (502-695-8881) at mile 16.5, and the Bluegrass Inn (502-695-1800) at mile 17.7. There are no campgrounds directly on the tour, but you can camp at the Kentucky Horse Park near Lexington or at the Elkhorn Campground just east of Frankfort.

20

Lower Kentucky Valley

■ **DISTANCE:** 47.8 miles

■ **HIGHLIGHTS:** River views and historic river ports

The Kentucky River cuts right through the Bluegrass from south-east to northwest. Most of the glory goes to the middle stretch (between Boonesborough and Frankfort), with its deep gorge and inaccessible cliffs. But the lower valley has its own quiet charm and is a lot easier to reach by bike. From Gratz down to the river's mouth in Carrollton, roads follow both banks. The roads never stray far from the river, and are often within sight of water.

The tour follows these two roads, making a long, thin loop. If you are tempted to shorten the loop by cutting across, forget it. You can't cross the river by bike anywhere between Gratz and Carrollton. If you start this ride, plan on going all the way around.

The floodplain within the valley supports crops, but farms here look a lot poorer than those in the Inner Bluegrass. Sheep and cattle outnumber thoroughbreds. And the region lies too far from big cities to attract many commuters or hobby farmers. Thanks to all those factors, the valley maintains a quiet, pastoral air that makes it a pleasure to cycle through. You can count on very light traffic, except for the ride through Carrollton and a short stretch along the east bank south of town.

The tour begins at General Butler State Park, just north of Exit 44 on I-71. This is a good choice if you are coming from Louisville, Cincinnati, or farther away. If you are driving in from Lexington or

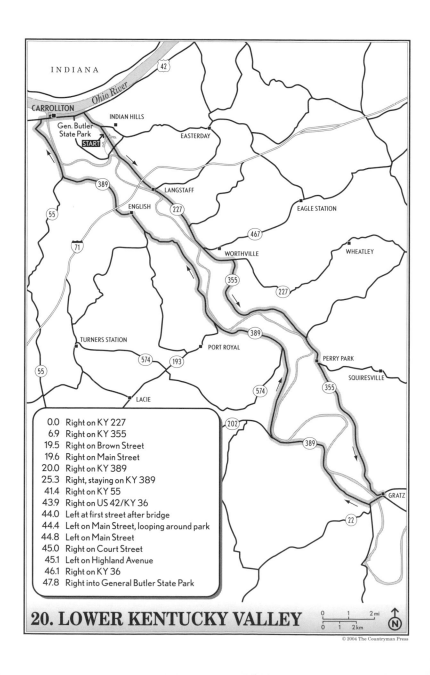

0.0	Right on KY 227
6.9	Right on KY 355
19.5	Right on Brown Street
19.6	Right on Main Street
20.0	Right on KY 389
25.3	Right, staying on KY 389
41.4	Right on KY 55
43.9	Right on US 42/KY 36
44.0	Left at first street after bridge
44.4	Left on Main Street, looping around park
44.8	Left on Main Street
45.0	Right on Court Street
45.1	Left on Highland Avenue
46.1	Right on KY 36
47.8	Right into General Butler State Park

20. LOWER KENTUCKY VALLEY

0   1   2 mi
0   1   2 km

N

Frankfort, it is easier to start in Gratz at mile 19.6. Park on the street there (you won't have any trouble finding a spot) near Webster's Grocery and Restaurant, and then head out across the bridge.

DIRECTIONS FOR THE RIDE

Start in the parking lot just inside the main entrance at General Butler State Park. The park has picnic tables, camping, and a lodge. It also offers mountain-bike trails, rare in the Bluegrass.

0.0 Right on KY 227.

0.9 Cross railroad tracks.
The crossing is smooth but diagonal, so take care.

1.9 Cross under I-71. Much of the traffic leaves here for the interstate.
A busy commercial district has grown up around the I-71 exit. It includes convenience stores, five hotels, and the usual complement of fast-food franchises—without which interstate drivers would, apparently, starve.

5.6 Pass KY 467.
A sign says WORTHVILLE BUSINESS DISTRICT, but these days the district includes nothing but a post office.
   I hesitate to recommend it, but a few readers may want to detour left on KY 467 to see Worthville. A railroad town through and through, it was laid out in 1867 when the Louisville, Cincinnati & Lexington Railway came through. The tracks still go through the center of town. Railroad construction and repair supplies are spread out on the ground beside the tracks, with just a few dozen modest houses in the area. And that's all there is to Worthville.

6.2 Enter Owen County as you cross Eagle Creek.

6.9 Right on KY 355.

10.6 Pass a dirt road that leads to Twin Eagles Wildlife Management Area, of interest mainly to hunters.

13.2 Cross Big Twin Creek.
A boat ramp here makes it easy to get a close view of the wide creek. Not far beyond the creek the road starts a long, stiff climb that takes you out of the valley

and up to the Bluegrass Plateau. The grade is steep, but it rewards you with high views of the river and valley.

17.8 Pass Fairview Market, a touristy store and restaurant.
You are still up on the plateau, but the thrilling descent to the town of Gratz starts a short way ahead. Get a good grip on the handlebars and enjoy the ride.

19.5 Right on Brown Street as you enter Gratz.
Gratz is a river port, a term that meant more a century ago than it does today. On the scale that runs from boomtown to ghost town, Gratz is pretty near the ghostly end. Still, it hangs on.

The town was laid out in 1847, though boats loaded cargo here even earlier. It took its name from the Gratz family, the first Jewish settlers to reach Kentucky. The town always depended on the river, and its fortunes rose and fell with the river traffic.

Commercial navigation on the Kentucky River was marginal in the best of

Downtown Carrollton.

times, and those times didn't last long. For most of the 19th century, shoals and snags severely limited steamboat travel. Eventually a series of locks and dams made the river navigable all the way up to Beattyville, but the last dam wasn't finished till 1917. By then, river traffic was already in decline. Railroads had reached the region and highways were starting to penetrate, siphoning off most of the freight and passengers. On top of that, the Kentucky River locks were smaller than those on the Ohio and Mississippi, and the channel was only 6 feet deep.

Even so, ports like Gratz had their day in the sun. In the early 20th century, small riverboats called packets stopped at Gratz for passengers and freight. Steam-powered packets ran till 1920, and gas-powered versions ran a few years longer. Travelers could go upstream to Frankfort and beyond or downstream to the big cities on the Ohio River. The Kentucky River even had its own show- boats—smaller versions of the floating palaces that plied the Mississippi. One showboat calling at Gratz advertised: "Did you ever see a whale!" For 15 cents each (a dime for kids), locals could see the preserved carcass of a 65-foot-long sea mammal.

You'll find no whales in Gratz today, though, and few boats use the river. But the town remains, and the river keeps flowing past the landing.

19.6 Right on Main Street.
Webster's Grocery and Restaurant stands at the corner. Though it offers the usual country-store fare, it looks like a city store, squeezed right up to the sidewalk like a shop in New York or Boston.

19.7 Cross the Kentucky River and enter Henry County.

20.0 Right on KY 389.

24.6 Pass a country store.

25.3 Right as KY 389 makes a sharp turn.

34.0 Enter Carroll County.

37.7 Cross railroad tracks and enter the village of English (no services).

38.5 Cross I-71.

41.4 Right on KY 55.

43.9 Right on US 42/KY 36.

There is a store on the northwest corner, and you may need it since the last one was almost 20 miles back. More stores are just ahead in Carrollton.

After the turn, cross the Kentucky River for the second and last time.

44.0 Left at the first street beyond the bridge.

You are now in Carrollton, Carroll County seat and the only substantial town on the Kentucky River below Frankfort. It dates from 1792 and used to be called Port William. The present name honors Charles Carroll, the longest-surviving signer of the Declaration of Independence.

44.4 Left on Main Street.

Make three right turns in a row, looping around a city park. The second turn, at the boat ramp, puts you a few steps from the Kentucky River's confluence with the much bigger Ohio. The park has picnic tables and public toilets.

44.8 Left on Main Street. This is the same corner you passed at mile 44.4, but you are now facing the opposite way.

Ahead lies the Carrollton historic district, with 26 buildings on the National Register. The old Carrollton Inn, on the right, is still open for meals and overnight stays.

45.0 Right on Court Street. Check out the tiny jail.

45.1 Left on Highland Avenue.

46.1 Right on KY 36. Keep right as KY 227 forks off.

47.8 Right into General Butler State Park and end at the parking lot.

Bicycle Shops

None. Take your tools.

Lodging

Five hotels—Best Western (502-732-8444), Days Inn (502-732-9301), Hampton Inn (502-732-0700), Holiday Inn (502-732-6661), and Super 8 (502-732-0252)—are clustered near the junction of KY 227 and I-71 at mile 1.9 on the tour (Exit 44 for I-71 freeway drivers). The old Carrollton Inn (502-732-6905) offers rooms in the heart of Carrollton's historic district at mile 44.9. General Butler State Park (502-732-4384), at the tour's start, has rooms, cabins, and campsites.

21

Following Daniel Boone

- **DISTANCE:** 49.4 miles
- **HIGHLIGHTS:** Reconstructed Fort Boonesborough, horse country, a ferry across the Kentucky River, and well-spaced country stores

Everyone who travels to Kentucky follows Daniel Boone, but this tour sticks particularly close to his actual route. When Boone arrived in Kentucky to settle (he had visited before to hunt and explore), he came up from Cumberland Gap on what became known as the Boone Trace. He started out on March 10, 1775, with 30 axmen to help cut the trail. They didn't blaze a new trail all the way, however. Boone and his crew followed existing trails and buffalo runs where they could.

The group set out on the Warriors' Path, used by Shawnee and Cherokee Indians traveling between Ohio and Tennessee. To the Indians, this trail was known as Athiamiowee. Boone entered the Bluegrass region a few miles east of present-day Berea. His luck ran out when he made camp on Taylor's Fork, close to the eventual site of Richmond. Indians attacked the party, killing two of Boone's men and wounding another. Boone pushed northward after that setback, going down Otter Creek to the Kentucky River, where he founded Boonesborough.

Otter Creek is where this tour picks up Boone's Trace. The last few miles of the ride follow the creek, just as Boone and his men did as they approached their destination. If you are not literally

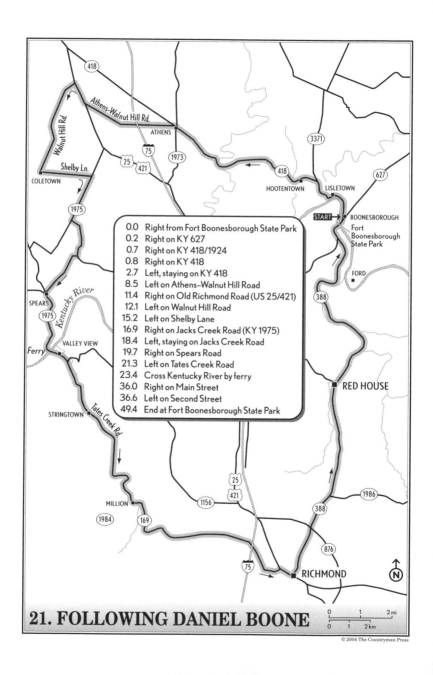

0.0	Right from Fort Boonesborough State Park
0.2	Right on KY 627
0.7	Right on KY 418/1924
0.8	Right on KY 418
2.7	Left, staying on KY 418
8.5	Left on Athens–Walnut Hill Road
11.4	Right on Old Richmond Road (US 25/421)
12.1	Left on Walnut Hill Road
15.2	Left on Shelby Lane
16.9	Right on Jacks Creek Road (KY 1975)
18.4	Left, staying on Jacks Creek Road
19.7	Right on Spears Road
21.3	Left on Tates Creek Road
23.4	Cross Kentucky River by ferry
36.0	Right on Main Street
36.6	Left on Second Street
49.4	End at Fort Boonesborough State Park

21. FOLLOWING DANIEL BOONE

© 2004 The Countryman Press

riding over Boone's footprints here, you're certainly close to them.

Boonesborough quickly became the base for settlement in the area. By 1790 it had over 100 houses. But despite its historic importance, it turned out to be a dud as a real town. Other places soon passed it in population, and by 1820 it had just about vanished. Eventually, local farmers took it over and plowed up the town streets for crops.

Boonesborough's rise and fall parallels that of Jamestown, the Virginia town settled in 1607. We honor and remember both towns for their roles in American history, but no one lives in either place anymore. The torch was passed on.

Daniel Boone moved on, too. He never spent much time at Boonesborough, and he left for good in 1783. Truth is, his restless nature kept him on the move for much of his life.

This is a longish ride, but it needs to be. If you want the complete Daniel Boone experience, you should put in some hard miles. Boone once covered 160 miles in four days on his way to warn Fort Boonesborough of a Shawnee attack. And he wasn't riding a bike.

Some stretches of this tour—though not the whole thing—are popular with Lexington's club cyclists. So you stand a better chance of encountering fellow cyclists on this tour than on most others in the book.

The tour starts and ends at Fort Boonesborough State Park, located in northern Madison County near Exit 95 on I-75. If you live in Lexington, you might want to start closer to home. One option is to drive to Jacobson Park on the southeast side of town, and park near the boat dock. When you ride out of the park, go straight through the traffic light and head out Old Richmond Road (US 25/421). In a mile you'll come to Walnut Hill Road, where you can turn right to join the tour at mile 12.1.

The city bus is another option for folks starting in Lexington. Ride the Number 6 bus out Richmond Road, getting off where the bus turns left at Eagle Creek Drive. Continue on Richmond Road by bike across the reservoir. Turn right on Old Richmond Road (US 25/421) and go a mile to Walnut Hill Road, where you again turn right to join the tour at mile 12.1.

The ride begins at the campground in Fort Boonesborough State Park. Not everyone likes camping, but a night or two on the ground here will help you appreciate what Boone and the other settlers did. Steer clear of the wide-open RV sites, which look barren and ugly. Head to the shady tenting area instead. Boone probably camped here, or very close by, when he first arrived. The campground is open year-round.

The campground sits next to the river, which has a sandy bank. It used to be a popular swimming beach, but the park authorities often banned swimming when pollution in the river grew too high. Eventually they built a big, fancy pool and closed the beach. You can still walk and sunbathe here, but you're supposed to stay out of the river.

From the beach you can see Lock and Dam Number 10. Like all Kentucky River locks above Frankfort, this one is no longer in use. The dam has structural problems and could fail disastrously if not repaired soon. The lockkeeper's house is in much better

Tates Creek Valley in Madison County.

shape than the lock and dam. Every lock used to have a similar house nearby, but this is the only one left.

The park's main feature is the reconstructed fort. A footpath (no bikes allowed) runs from the campground up the hill to the fort. You can ride your bike to the fort, but the road is much longer than the footpath. It's an easy walk, anyway.

The fort contains cabins and workshops where people dressed like pioneers demonstrate candle making, spinning, and other crafts. The fort displays several monumental oil paintings; my favorite shows Boone and his cohorts on Pilot Knob, viewing the Bluegrass for the first time.

DIRECTIONS FOR THE RIDE

Start at the campground driveway in Fort Boonesborough State Park.

0.0 Right as you leave the campground.

0.2 Right on KY 627, which has a paved shoulder.

0.6 Cross the Kentucky River and enter Clark County. (The ride started in Madison County.)
Look upstream to see Lock and Dam Number 10.

0.7 Right on KY 418/1924.

0.8 Right on KY 418 as it splits from KY 1924. Pass under the bridge.
The road passes two riverside taverns on the left and several small waterfalls on the right. The falls dry up at times.

At mile 1.7 an abandoned quarry cuts into the bluffs. The quarry is fenced off, but even from outside the fence you can get a good geology lesson. The Bluegrass region's limestone foundation is laid out here in all its glory. Some of the layers have a distinctly bluish cast. In the past, some people claimed that the blue limestone was responsible for the color of Kentucky bluegrass. But that seems unlikely—especially in view of the fact that most honest observers admit that Kentucky bluegrass is really green.

2.0 Pass Hall's on the River, a popular restaurant.
Beyond Hall's the road crosses a mini-gorge and starts a big climb. This is the steepest hill you will face today.

2.7 Left at fork, staying on KY 418.
Shearer's Corner Market, the first country store of the tour, is located here.

In the perfect cycling world, a country store would pop up every few miles. On this ride it actually happens. Stores appear at miles 2.7, 8.3, 21.4, 28.1, and 42.8. And that's not counting the abundance of stores as you pass through Richmond.

5.2 Cross Grimes Mill Road.
A left here would take you to one of the steepest roads in the Bluegrass. But you have miles to go, so you had better save that hill for another day. (Ride 8 goes there.)

6.4 Cross Boone Creek and enter Fayette County.
Kayakers consider this creek one of the best whitewater streams in the state, but it's only runnable a couple of days a year.

8.4 Cross Cleveland Road in downtown Athens. There is a small grocery store here.
Lexington used to bill itself as the "Athens of the West," and somehow that name became attached to this tiny village several miles southwest of Lexington. Comparing this place (or even Lexington) to the noble Greek city is a stretch. But if Georgia can have its Rome and Illinois its Cairo, why not?

Before it got the name Athens, this village was called Cross Plains for the two buffalo runs that crossed here.

8.5 Left on Athens–Walnut Hill Road.

9.6 Cross over I-75.

11.4 Right on Old Richmond Road (US 25/421).
Traffic can be heavy here.

12.1 Left on Walnut Hill Road.
For the next few miles, the road passes several horse farms.

If you started in Lexington, either by parking your car at Jacobson Park or by riding the bus out Richmond Road, this is where you get off. Don't turn left on Walnut Hill Road; just continue on Old Richmond Road.

14.8 Enter Coletown (no services).

15.2 Left on Shelby Lane.

16.9 Right on Jacks Creek Road (KY 1975).

18.4 Left at the intersection with Crawley Lane. Stay on Jacks Creek Road as it turns left.

19.7 Right on Spears Road. KY 1975 makes the turn with you.

21.3 Left on Tates Creek Road at the T-junction.

21.4 Enter Spears as KY 169, coming in from the right, joins Tates Creek Road.
This village has two stores. The Country Store, loaded with atmosphere, is on the left. A bigger, more modern store is to the right. The modern store is probably the place to go if you need a head of lettuce or a package of hot dogs. But the Country Store is the normal stop for local cyclists, who often ride this road.

Beyond Spears the road starts a 2-mile descent into the Kentucky River Gorge.

23.4 Cross the Kentucky River and enter Madison County on the Valley View Ferry. It's free.
Ferries have been running here since 1785, when the Virginia government (Kentucky hadn't achieved statehood yet) licensed John Craig to start one. The paddle wheel that powers you across is supposed to be a century old. The boat itself is a lot newer and meets the same safety standards as any other American ferry. The ferry runs seven days a week, but has been known to shut down for high water and repairs. Call 859-258-3611 to see whether it's running when you need it.

A small park overlooks the ferry landing from the Fayette County side. It has picnic tables and a tower that shows the high-water marks from all the great floods.

As you ride the ferry, look right for the steel piers of the long-gone railroad bridge. A beloved local railroad, the Richmond, Nicholasville, Irvine & Beattyville, crossed the river here. Everybody called it the Riney-B.

23.5 Enter Valley View (no services).
Tates Creek Road (KY 169) continues into Madison County, with a pleasant sur-prise. After the steep descent from Spears to the ferry landing, you have every rea-son to expect a hard climb on the other side. But that hard climb never materi-alizes. Instead, the road follows Tates Creek to Richmond, climbing gently all the way. The creek, carving its course over thousands of years, has provided an easy way up the hill.

It also offers great scenery. The Tates Creek Valley is a feast for the eyes, with narrow farms tucked between steep hills. When I first came here I assumed that

Valley View got its name from the Kentucky River Valley. Now I prefer to think, rightly or wrongly, that it refers to the Tates Creek Valley.

28.0 Cross Whitlock Road (KY 1985), which comes in from the right.
From here you can see the Little Ferry Market, another of those well-spaced country stores.

29.8 Enter the village of Million, named for a local landowner (no services).

30.9 Pass more ruins of the Riney-B Railroad.

34.7 Cross under I-75 and enter Richmond.
Tates Creek still flows next to the road, but it's so narrow this far upstream that you can jump across.

35.9 Pass the entrance to E. C. Million Memorial Park, which has picnic tables.

36.0 Right on Main Street.
Downtown Richmond is just ahead, with restaurants and stores.

36.5 Cross Third Street and pass the Glyndon Hotel.

36.6 Left on Second Street, just short of the courthouse. Maps show this as KY 388, but there's no sign downtown to mark it.

37.1 Cross railroad tracks.
From here the road leaves Richmond by way of an industrial area, passing the Daniel Boone Elementary School. What were they thinking, naming a school for old Dan'l? By all accounts, he neither liked school nor attended it much.

37.6 Pass the last Richmond store before heading out into the country.

38.3 Cross under the Eastern Bypass, KY 876.

42.6 Cross under railroad.

42.7 Cross Otter Creek.
Boone and his fellow trailblazers followed this creek on their way to Boonesborough.

42.8 Enter the village of Red House, where you'll find a country store.

46.6 Cross railroad tracks.

46.7 Cross Otter Creek again.
The road on the right leads to Otter Creek Campsite and Canoe Rental.

49.1 Enter Fort Boonesborough State Park.

49.4 Right into the park campground to end the ride.

Bicycle Shops

Dodds Cyclery, 1985 Harrodsburg Road, Lexington; 859-277-6013

Pedal Power, 401 South Upper Street, Lexington; 859-255-6408

Scheller's, 212 Woodland Avenue, Lexington; 859-233-1764

Vicious Cycle, Todds Road at Codell, Lexington; 859-263-7300

Lodging

The Glyndon Hotel (859-623-1224) in downtown Richmond is at mile 36.5 of the tour. Off route, you can find all kinds of hotels and motels in Richmond and Lexington. The campground at Fort Boonesborough State Park is open year-round and puts you right at the starting point. That's hard to beat.

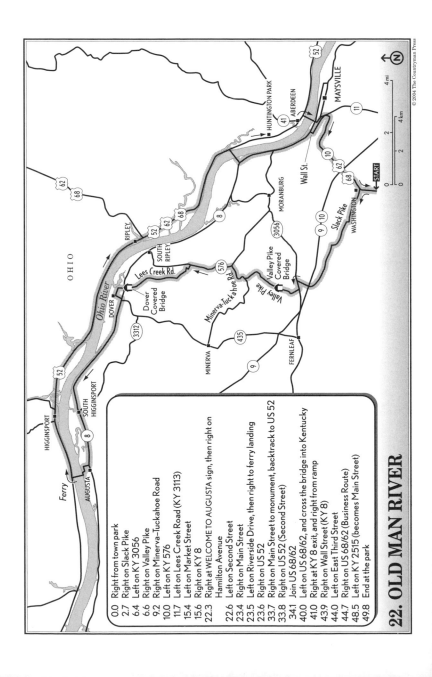

0.0 Right from town park
2.7 Right on Slack Pike
6.4 Left on KY 3056
6.6 Right on Valley Pike
9.2 Right on Minerva–Tuckahoe Road
10.0 Left on KY 576
11.7 Left on Lees Creek Road (KY 3113)
15.4 Left on Market Street
15.6 Right on KY 8
22.3 Right at WELCOME TO AUGUSTA sign, then right on Hamilton Avenue
22.6 Left on Second Street
23.4 Right on Main Street
23.5 Left on Riverside Drive, then right to ferry landing
23.6 Right on US 52
33.7 Right on Main Street to monument, backtrack to US 52
33.8 Right on US 52 (Second Street)
34.1 Join US 68/62
40.0 Left on US 68/62, and cross the bridge into Kentucky
41.0 Right at KY 8 exit, and right from ramp
43.9 Right on Wall Street (KY 8)
44.0 Left on East Third Street
44.7 Right on US 68/62 (Business Route)
48.5 Left on KY 2515 (becomes Main Street)
49.8 End at the park

22. OLD MAN RIVER

© 2004 The Countryman Press

Old Man River

- **DISTANCE:** 49.8 miles
- **HIGHLIGHTS:** Two covered bridges, a ferry, Ohio River views, and Underground Railroad historic sites

This tour is really two rides in one. Part one takes you through a rolling countryside of small farms and woods—a typical Outer Bluegrass landscape. The second part follows the Ohio River through the old port towns of Augusta, Ripley, and Maysville. You cross the Ohio twice—first on a small ferry and later on a new cable-stayed bridge.

The terrain is hilly in the first part but almost dead level along the Ohio River. There is one tough climb near the end as you leave the Ohio Valley and return to the Bluegrass Plateau, so save some energy for it.

The Ohio Valley is part of the Bluegrass, but peeks out at the wider world up and down the mighty river. The towns here look different from most others around the state. Row houses are common, and some neighborhoods would seem right at home in Pittsburgh, 400 miles upriver.

This tour is almost exactly 50 miles long, making it a good choice for a half-century ride.

DIRECTIONS FOR THE RIDE

Start at a town park at the south end of Washington, just off US 68/62. The park has picnic tables and a small lake and is popular with local runners. It closes at 10 PM, so park outside the gate if you think you might get back late.

0.0 Right on leaving the park.

0.7 Enter downtown Washington.
Little more than a village, the town developed very early in Kentucky's history. And then nothing much happened for 200 years. Most towns this old have seen their original architecture replaced by modern buildings, but Washington maintained its early look. Today it resembles Colonial Williamsburg—more a museum than a real, working town. But it's a nice museum, with log buildings and brick houses from the late 18th century.

1.3 Cross US 68/62.

2.7 Right on Slack Pike.

5.9 Cross AA Highway.
A truck stop to the right offers food and drink. It's not much, but you'll find nothing better till you reach Augusta 17 miles ahead.

6.4 Left on KY 3056 (not marked) where Slack Pike ends at a T-junction.
A closed gas station is on the right.

6.6 Right on Valley Pike at the black barn.

8.1 Look right for the Valley Pike covered bridge, on a gravel lane just off the paved road.
Look hard or you'll miss it, because this is the shortest covered bridge in Kentucky. It looks like a one-car garage that happens to span a creek. The gravel lane is ride-able, but you should dismount before crossing the bridge. The bridge deck is short a few boards and has nails sticking up. Some of Kentucky's covered bridges are lovingly maintained; unfortunately, this is not one of them. You have to wonder how much longer it will last.

9.2 Right on Minerva–Tuckahoe Road at the T-junction.

10.0 Left on KY 576 at the T-junction.

11.7 Left on Lees Creek Road (KY 3113). The intersection is poorly marked.
From here to mile 13.0 enjoy the marvelous downhill run. The road is only one lane wide, and dense forest presses in on both sides. You could easily hit 35 mph but

Kentucky's smallest covered bridge.

probably shouldn't, since the pavement is not up to the usual Bluegrass standards. Washouts have been patched with loose gravel. I've encountered deer and free-ranging chickens on this road—all the more reason to keep your speed down.

14.7 Reach the day's second covered bridge.
The Dover Bridge lies right on the main route and is in superb condition. I still recommend that you walk across unless you are very skilled at riding narrow planks. Australian cyclists often talk about "pick-a-plank" bridges. You pick a plank and stay on it all the way across. If your tire slips off and catches between planks, you won't be happy.

14.8 Cross KY 8. Lees Creek Road becomes Johnson Street as you enter the village of Dover.

15.4 Left on Market Street.

15.6 Right on KY 8.
You are now in the Ohio Valley. Bluffs are visible right and left, but you don't get a good view of the mighty river itself till mile 17.9. Don't worry. Better river views are coming later in the trip.

22.3 Right at the WELCOME TO AUGUSTA sign. Turn right again almost immediately on Hamilton Avenue, at the Clopay factory.

22.6 Left on Second Street.
If you go straight instead you will enter Augusta River Park, a good place to fill water bottles or eat a picnic lunch while watching the river barges go by.

23.4 Right on Main Street in downtown Augusta.
This is one of the prettiest downtowns in all the Bluegrass, with restored shop fronts and a main street that goes right down to the river. You may have seen downtown Augusta at the movies. It played the roles of Hannibal, Missouri, in Huck Finn *and St. Louis in* Centennial.

23.5 Left on Riverside Drive, then immediately bear right to the ferry landing.
Augusta's visitors center is at the corner of Main and Riverside. If you plan to explore the town, this is a good place to start. The ferry runs whenever a customer shows up. Cars sometimes back up on the ramp but there's always room for a bike, so don't be shy about riding to the head of the line.

23.6 Right on US 52 at the top of the ramp as you leave the ferry.
*You are now in the state of Ohio. In the bad old days, runaway slaves who made
it this far knew they were close to freedom. You may feel a touch of freedom, too,
when you see what US 52 has to offer. It sprouts an appendage rarely seen in
Kentucky: a paved shoulder. It's not the world's smoothest or widest shoulder, but it
remains a constant friend (save a few blocks as you go through towns) till you cross
back into Kentucky.*

*The road is marked as a scenic highway and lives up to its billing. It runs very
close to the river (closer than KY 8 on the opposite bank) and provides many good
views.*

25.6 Enter Higginsport.
*The town offers restaurants and a grocery store, and there is a park with picnic
tables at mile 26.1.*

26.7 Pass the entrance to the White Oak Campground.
The campground caters mainly to RV travelers, but bike tourists are also welcome.

33.0 Enter Ripley.
*The town looks more substantial than its population—under 2,000—would sug-
gest. Ripley was a key station on the Underground Railroad, the network of safe
houses and secret routes that helped runaway slaves reach freedom in the northern states and Canada. Over 2,000 slaves passed through this area.*

*Some of the most active abolitionists lived here. Two of the best known were
John Rankin and John Parker, and you can visit their houses.*

33.7 Right on Main Street.
*Main Street ends at the river, one block south. A monument to local abolitionists
and Civil War heroes stands here. Civil War monuments are a dime a dozen, but
monuments to abolitionists are rare. If any town should have one, it's Ripley.*

Make a U-turn at the monument and go back to US 52.

33.8 Right on US 52, here called Second Street.
*Check out the unusual Carnegie Library on the southeast corner. Most of these
libraries are neoclassical with stone columns. Ripley's library, in contrast, was built
in prairie style (think Frank Lloyd Wright, though this particular example was
designed by H. T. Liebert), with ribbon windows and a low red roof. A mark near
the front door shows how high the Ohio River rose in 1937. It's scary to think the
water could rise to that level again; yet it surely will.*

34.1 Join US 68/62, which comes in from the left.
You'll face more traffic from here to the Ohio River bridge.

40.0 Left on US 68/62 as those routes peel off from US 52. Follow the loop to the William H. Hanska Bridge over the Ohio River.
Open only since 2001, it was Kentucky's first cable-stayed bridge and has a 1,050-foot main span. Big bridges can be scary, but this one has a nice wide shoulder.

41.0 Right at the exit for KY 8. Turn right again at the bottom of the ramp.

43.2 Enter the outskirts of Maysville.
This is one of the oldest towns in Kentucky. It was an important port of entry for settlers who arrived via the Ohio River.

43.9 Right on Wall Street, staying on KY 8.

44.0 Left on East Third Street at the top of the hill.
The National Underground Railroad Museum is at 115 East Third Street. It's open 10–4 every day but Sunday. Like Ripley across the river, Maysville was an important stop for slaves heading north. Unlike Ripley, Maysville, home to both slave traders and abolitionists, was part of Kentucky, where slavery was legal and helping a slave escape was not. Ask at the museum about nearby sites related to the Underground Railroad. The house called Phillip's Folly is worth a look.

44.3 Cross Market Street. Downtown Maysville is on your left.

44.7 Right on US 68/62 (Business Route). There is a small park to the right as you make the turn.
The next mile and a half challenges you with the toughest climb of the tour, and one of the toughest anywhere in the Bluegrass. Settlers who arrived by boat had to struggle up this hill. It sometimes took a whole day. You will undoubtedly climb it a lot faster—but then you aren't carrying all your possessions with you. When you pull abreast of McDonald's, the worst of the grade is behind you. You have now regained the Bluegrass Plateau.

47.5 Cross AA Highway.
This is a busy commercial area, with restaurants and a big modern supermarket.

48.5 Left on KY 2515. The road curves right to become Main Street in Washington.

49.8 End the tour back at the park.

Bicycle Shops

Pedalsmith, 8 East Third Street, Maysville; 606-563-0420

Lodging

Maysville has several motels, including a Super 8 (606-759-8888) just 2 miles north of the start. You can also camp at Blue Licks State Park (859-289-5507) 18 miles south, and at several spots along US 52 in Ohio.

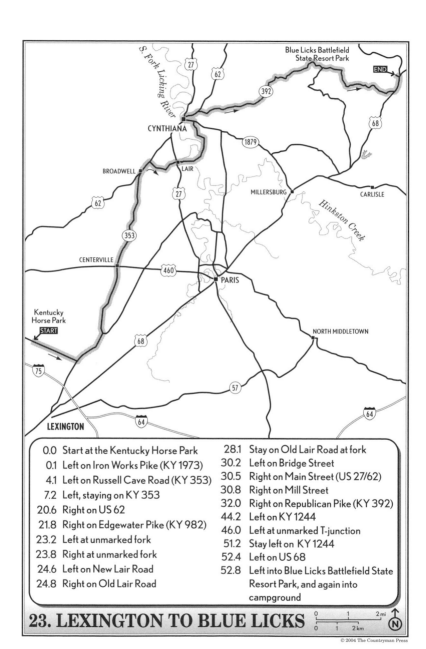

Blue Licks Battlefield
State Resort Park

END

CYNTHIANA

BROADWELL   LAIR

MILLERSBURG   CARLISLE

Hinkston Creek

CENTERVILLE

PARIS

Kentucky
Horse Park
START

NORTH MIDDLETOWN

LEXINGTON

0.0 Start at the Kentucky Horse Park	28.1 Stay on Old Lair Road at fork
0.1 Left on Iron Works Pike (KY 1973)	30.2 Left on Bridge Street
4.1 Left on Russell Cave Road (KY 353)	30.5 Right on Main Street (US 27/62)
7.2 Left, staying on KY 353	30.8 Right on Mill Street
20.6 Right on US 62	32.0 Right on Republican Pike (KY 392)
21.8 Right on Edgewater Pike (KY 982)	44.2 Left on KY 1244
23.2 Left at unmarked fork	46.0 Left at unmarked T-junction
23.8 Right at unmarked fork	51.2 Stay left on KY 1244
24.6 Left on New Lair Road	52.4 Left on US 68
24.8 Right on Old Lair Road	52.8 Left into Blue Licks Battlefield State Resort Park, and again into campground

23. LEXINGTON TO BLUE LICKS

0   1   2 mi
0   1   2 km

N

Lexington to Blue Licks

- **DISTANCE:** 52.9 miles
- **HIGHLIGHTS:** Horse country near Lexington, the Licking River (the South and Main Forks), and Blue Licks Battlefield State Park

The trip starts amid the famous horse farms of the Inner Blue-grass. You then cross the South Fork of the Licking River near Cynthiana and head out into the wild woods of the Eden Shale Belt. Near the end you cross the mainstem Licking River before rolling into the park at Blue Licks.

Blue Licks was the last battle of the American Revolution. Growing up in eastern Virginia, I was taught that the Battle of Yorktown ended the Revolution. And so it did, as far as the big armies were concerned. But there was no peace treaty for almost two years after Cornwallis surrendered at Yorktown. During those two years, skirmishes continued along the western frontier. The skirmishes always involved Indians, and some historians believe the conflict had less to do with the Revolution than with the continuing rivalry between Indians and Anglo-American settlers.

The Battle of Blue Licks was one of those skirmishes, but it was bigger than most. It was also a huge defeat for the Americans. It started when British and Indian fighters attacked Bryant's Station, a fortified settlement a few miles northeast of Lexington. About 360 men took part in the attack. Failing to capture the station, they gave up and headed back north.

That could have been the end of the affair, but Kentucky militiamen were already rushing to defend Bryant's Station. By the time they got there the British and Indians had left, but the Kentuckians were in no mood to let them go without a fight. About 180 men of the Fayette County militia took off after the enemy, unwilling to wait for reinforcements that were soon to arrive. Among the group were Daniel Boone and his son, Israel.

The militiamen caught sight of the British and Indians near Blue Licks, where a ford crossed the Licking River. The Americans were still south of the river and their foes north of it. Knowing the steep terrain ahead and fearing an ambush, Boone advised caution. Several officers argued they should wait for reinforcements. That would have been a wise decision, but a few hotblooded young men chose for themselves and charged across the ford. The rest of the Americans had no real choice but to follow, and so the battle began. It turned out to be an ambush, just as Boone had feared. The fighting lasted only minutes, but when it ended almost half the Kentuckians were dead, including Israel Boone. The British and Indians lost fewer than a dozen men.

A few days later the reinforcements—about 500 men—arrived at Blue Licks. But the battle was over, and all that remained was to bury the dead and argue about what went wrong.

This tour generally follows the route taken by the Kentucky militia in chasing the British and Indians. Like the militiamen, you start in Fayette County and finish at the battlefield. Unlike them, you won't face deadly fire when you get there. Instead, you will find a pleasant state park with a campground and lodge.

The tour begins and ends at state park campgrounds, making it ideal for bicycle camping. If you aren't camping, you may want to adjust those points. You could start at Exit 115 on I-75, where you can pick from four modern hotels. From there, bike north on Newtown Pike for 2.2 miles. Turn right on Iron Works Pike and pick up the tour at mile 1.7. At the other end, in Blue Licks, just shoot past the campground and stay at the lodge or in one of the cabins.

This is a one-way trip, which leads to the question of how you get back to Lexington if that's your home or where you left your car.

The Jot 'Em Down Store in Fayette County.

There is, alas, no bus service. One solution is to persuade someone to drive you back. Another is to turn around and retrace the outbound route, though that's a long ride. A third option is to head back the short way on US 68, the normal motor route between Blue Licks and Lexington. I've ridden US 68 and I'd do it again, but I hesitate to recommend it since it is a busy, mostly shoulderless road. The stretch from Millersburg to Paris is no fun at all.

DIRECTIONS FOR THE RIDE

0.0 Start at the campground entrance of the Kentucky Horse Park.

0.1 Left on Iron Works Pike (KY 1973).
Turning right here instead of left would take you to the Kentucky Horse Park's main entrance. The park is worth a visit, but you had better arrive a day before your trip if you want to do it justice. You could easily spend a whole day here.

1.7 Cross Newtown Pike (KY 922).
If you started from Exit 115 on I-75, where all the hotels are, this is where you join the tour.

4.1 Left on Russell Cave Road (KY 353).
The Jot 'Em Down Store is located here. (See Ride 14 for more information on the store.)
    At mile 4.6 the road reaches the great Mount Brilliant Horse Farm. Russell Cave is located here. Look left to see the cave entrance, where prehistoric bones have turned up. It's more than just a cave, however. Political picnics used to be held here, and in 1843 it was the scene of a fight between Samuel Brown and Cassius Marcellus Clay, an anti-slavery politician who later played a key role in buying Alaska from the Russians. When I call it a fight, I'm not speaking figuratively. Brown, who may have been a hired assassin, shot at Clay, who fought back with his long knife. He fatally wounded Brown and threw him into the pond. Kentucky politics have long been, well, interesting.

7.2 Left at the fork, staying on KY 353.

10.7 Pass the Loradale Grocery.
If you come through around lunchtime, get in line with the horse-farm workers and order a hot meal.

11.7 Enter Bourbon County.
This county took its name from the French royal family, and lent it to the famous whiskey.

12.3 Enter Centerville.
Opinions differ on what the town is actually the center of, but it is about midway between Lexington and Cynthiana.

12.7 Cross US 460.
A country store occupies the southeast corner.

16.5 Cross Silas Road and enter Jacksonville (no services).

18.2 Cross Silas Creek and enter Harrison County.

20.6 Right on US 62.
This is the main road into Cynthiana and may be a bit too busy for comfortable riding. But don't worry. Our route leaves it after only a mile and a half, heading into Cynthiana by the back door.

21.8 Right on Edgewater Pike (KY 982).

23.2 Left at an unmarked fork.

23.8 Right at another unmarked fork.

24.5 Cross US 27, a main highway.

24.6 Left on New Lair Road.

24.8 Right on Old Lair Road and cross under the railroad tracks.

24.9 Cross the South Fork of the Licking River.
The view here is superb.

28.1 Stay on Old Lair Road at the fork.

29.6 Enter Cynthiana.
There is no welcome sign on this back road, but when you see houses all around you know you have arrived. The street continues to be known as Old Lair Road.

*   More than one town has been named for a girl, but Cynthiana is the only town I know named for two girls. Robert Harrison, who donated the land for the town, had daughters named Cynthia and Anna. I guess he loved them both equally.*

30.2 Left on Bridge Street, where there is a supermarket.

30.4 Cross rough railroad tracks.

30.5 Right on Main Street (US 26/62), which heads through downtown Cynthiana.

30.8 Right on Mill Street as US 62 splits from US 27.

30.9 Cross railroad tracks.

31.6 Pass a small grocery store.
This is the last place to buy supplies before you reach Blue Licks. You are heading into the Eden Shale Belt, where people and stores are few.

32.0 Right on Republican Pike (KY 392).

39.7 Enter Buena Vista (no services).
So far KY 392 has more or less kept to the ridges. Beyond Buena Vista the road drops down to the valley and follows Pretty Branch for a while. The sharp transition from ridge to valley road is characteristic of the hilly Eden Shale Belt. You find few moderate slopes here. It's either level riding along ridge or creek or a steep pitch as the road shifts between the two. Somewhere near here the road enters Nicholas County, but no one bothered to put up a sign.

44.2 Left on KY 1244, which isn't marked in this direction. After making the turn, look over your shoulder for the KY 392 sign to confirm your location.

46.0 Left at an unmarked T-junction.

47.4 Stay on KY 1244 as it curves left.

50.0 Start a steep climb to the ridgetop.

51.2 Left at a T-junction. Leave KY 1244 here and ride the winding road down into the Licking Valley.

52.0 Cross the Licking River Main Fork on a one-lane bridge.
The bridge consists of two steel truss spans on piers made of stone and concrete. Off to the right you can see the new high-level bridge where US 68 crosses the Licking.

The village of Blue Licks is on the north bank of the river. Buffalo used to visit the area to lick the salt. Over the years this spot has gone by many names: the

Spring, Down at the Licks, the Salt Works, Blue Lick Springs, and Lower Blue Licks—a lot of names for a place that never had that many people. Not much remains now, but from 1860 to about 1900 a health resort operated here. Water from the spring was bottled and sold.

Next there's a hill to climb, of course, but it's mild compared to the steep roads of the Kentucky River Gorge. Though the Licking is a big river, its valley is much shallower than the Kentucky's.

52.4 Left on US 68, a busy two-lane road.
You can't easily ride the shoulder because the road builders have ruined it with deep rumble strips.

52.5 Enter Robertson County.

52.8 Left into Blue Licks Battlefield State Resort Park and left again to the campground.

52.9 End at the campground entrance.

Bicycle Shops

Dodds Cyclery, 1985 Harrodsburg Road, Lexington; 859-277-6013

Pedal Power, 401 South Upper Street, Lexington; 859-255-6408

Scheller's, 212 Woodland Avenue, Lexington; 859-233-1764

Vicious Cycle, Todds Road at Codell, Lexington; 859-263-7300

Pedalsmith, 8 East Third Street, Maysville; 606-563-0420

Lodging

At the Lexington end, you can camp at the Kentucky Horse Park or stay in comfort at Knights Inn (859-231-0232), Holiday Inn (859-233-0512), La Quinta (859-231-7551), or Four Points (859-259-1311) at Exit 115 on I-75. At Blue Licks State Park (859-289-5507), you can choose from campsites, rooms at the lodge, and cabins.

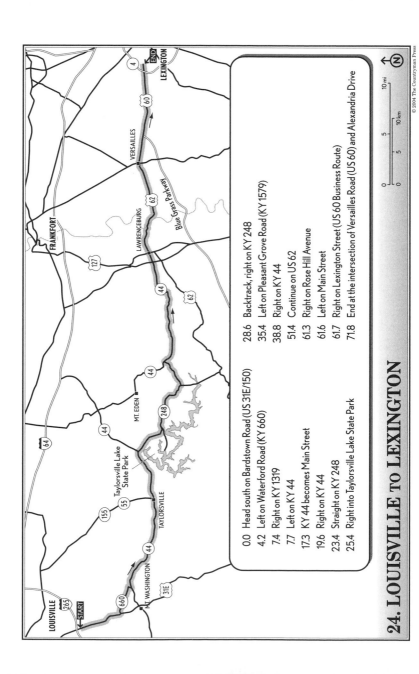

24. LOUISVILLE TO LEXINGTON

0.0	Head south on Bardstown Road (US 31E/150)
4.2	Left on Waterford Road (KY 660)
7.4	Right on KY 1319
7.7	Left on KY 44
17.3	KY 44 becomes Main Street
19.6	Right on KY 44
23.4	Straight on KY 248
25.4	Right into Taylorsville Lake State Park
28.6	Backtrack, right on KY 248
35.4	Left on Pleasant Grove Road (KY 1579)
38.8	Right on KY 44
51.4	Continue on US 62
61.3	Right on Rose Hill Avenue
61.6	Left on Main Street
61.7	Right on Lexington Street (US 60 Business Route)
71.8	End at the intersection of Versailles Road (US 60) and Alexandria Drive

24

Louisville to Lexington

- **DISTANCE:** 71.8 miles
- **HIGHLIGHTS:** Taylorsville Lake, the Kentucky River Gorge, and the many attractions in Kentucky's two biggest cities

You can drive from Louisville to Lexington in less than two hours, but that's no fun. This tour takes a slower and more interesting route between the two great cities of the Bluegrass. It starts in suburban Louisville in the Outer Bluegrass, but quickly leaves the city behind. In Spencer County the route goes through the town of Taylorsville and Taylorsville Lake State Park. In Anderson County you ride the ridges of the Eden Shale Belt and then follow the Salt River Valley before crossing the Kentucky River Gorge on a high bridge. The last few miles take you through the horse country of the Inner Bluegrass. The tour ends in suburban Lexington, close to the Keeneland Race Course.

This is another one-way ride. I describe it going from Louisville to Lexington. You can, of course, reverse the direction and start in Lexington, but I recommend against that because the scenery unfolds better west to east.

Picking the ideal start and end points was difficult, and you may want to adjust them for your ride. I was tempted to plot a route from city center to city center, but that would have meant miles of riding on city streets that are far from anyone's definition of a back road. I considered going from airport to airport, but that created some problems at the Louisville end. In the end I based my choice on city bus routes. The ride starts at a bus stop in Louisville and ends at a bus stop in Lexington.

Bus connections make it possible to arrange the whole trip without using a car. Take the Greyhound to Louisville and ride the local Number 17 to the end of the line. Then bike to Lexington, where you pick up the Number 4 bus. Lexington buses take you to the Greyhound station, and then you're on your way back home.

Some riders can do this distance in one day, but it's possible to make a good two days of it if you carry camping gear and stay at Taylorsville Lake State Park.

DIRECTIONS FOR THE RIDE

Start at the intersection of Bardstown Road (US 31E/150) and Glenmary Farm Drive. It's about a mile south of Exit 17 on I-65. Louisville's Number 17 bus serves this spot. If you plan to take the bus, call 502-585-1234 a day ahead and ask that they send a bus fitted with a bike rack. They'll do it on request.

0.0 South on Bardstown Road.
This is a busy four-lane divided highway with wide, paved shoulders. Traffic can be heavy here, but the shoulder keeps you clear of it.

3.6 Cross Floyds Fork, a tributary of the Salt River, after a good downhill run.

4.2 Left on Waterford Road (KY 660).
Say good-bye to the busy highway and paved shoulder. This road gets some commuter traffic, but apart from rush hour it should be pretty quiet.

4.7 Enter Bullitt County.

7.4 Right on KY 1319.

7.7 Left on KY 44 at a T-junction.

8.4 Pass a tavern.

8.8 Enter Spencer County.

12.2 Enter the village of Waterford.
The store here has closed, and you'll find no other stores or restaurants before

Taylorsville. But there is a community park at mile 12.4, just past the creek.

17.3 Pass the intersection with KY 1633 and enter Taylorsville. KY 44 becomes Main Street.

18.0 Straight on Main Street as KY 44 heads off to the left.
There is a variety store at the corner. This is the old road out of town, now called KY 3200. You have a bit of a climb ahead as you leave Taylorsville.

19.6 Right on KY 44, which has become a four-lane divided road with paved shoulders.

20.1 Pass the Lakeside Restaurant, which has a motel.

20.4 Pass a country store.

23.4 Straight on KY 248 as KY 44 branches off to the left.
The four-lane road with paved shoulders continues.

25.4 Right into Taylorsville Lake State Park. If you don't care to visit the park, just go straight and save 3 miles.
Taylorsville Lake is the biggest body of water in the Bluegrass. Like all lakes in these parts, it is artificial and not very old. The U.S. Army Corps of Engineers created it in 1982 by damming the Salt River. If you are spending the night here, you might want to check out the dam and visitors center located west of the park.

There is a nice new campground (closed in winter) and several miles of multi-use trails suitable for mountain bikes. Please note that while Kentucky law doesn't require bike helmets on public roads, park rules call for helmets on the off-road trails. Be advised that people ride horses on these trails, too, so make sure to give them the right-of-way.

26.9 Right at the park campground.

27.0 Left as you leave the campground.

28.6 Right on KY 248.
Within a quarter mile the four lanes shrink to two, and within a mile the paved shoulder dwindles to a few inches outside the paint stripe.

30.2 Pass a country store.

34.5 Enter Anderson County.

35.4 Left on Pleasant Grove Road (KY 1579).
From here to KY 44 the road follows a ridge. That's a common practice here in the Eden Shale Belt, where the land slopes too much for roads to cut straight across the terrain. The ridge road makes for good views and an easy ride.

38.8 Right on KY 44.
After a fast descent the road enters the Salt River Valley. The view here is picture-perfect: a narrow, fertile valley framed by steep hills.

41.2 Enter Glenboro.
There are no services here except for a couple of soda machines.

46.1 Cross Drydock Road, which heads off to the right.
The Salt River comes right up to KY 44 here, and a very short detour down Drydock Road gives you a close look at it.

Just beyond Drydock Road there is an old, abandoned distillery. Anderson County still has two working distilleries, and you'll pass one down the road.

47.5 Cross Hammond Creek.

A bourbon distillery at the Kentucky River Gorge.

Watch out for diagonal bridge joints, which can throw you. Just as at railroad tracks that cross the road diagonally, the best course is to slow down and steer so you cross the joints at right angles.

50.5 Cross the Lawrenceburg Bypass. The main route goes straight.
If you turn right instead, in about a mile you will reach Lawrenceburg's main shopping district.

50.8 Pass a grocery store.
You can see downtown Lawrenceburg, dominated by the domed tower of the Anderson County Courthouse.

51.4 Cross Main Street in downtown Lawrenceburg.
Downtown is to your right, with several restaurants. Continue out of town on Woodford Street. KY 44 ends here, and the tour continues on US 62.

51.6 Cross railroad tracks.

52.0 Pass a small shopping center with two convenience stores.

53.9 Pass the Wild Turkey bourbon distillery and start the descent into the Kentucky River Gorge.

54.5 Cross the Kentucky River on the Blackburn Memorial Bridge.
This impressive bridge was built in 1932, but an even greater span stands next to it. Young's High Bridge dates from 1889. When built, it was the longest and highest steel cantilever bridge in America. Sad to say, it's no longer in use. The last passenger train crossed Young's High Bridge in 1937. Freight trains used it till 1985.

The track heading west to Lawrenceburg has been partly dismantled and is unlikely to open again. The track east to Versailles is still intact, however, and just possibly could be used for a scenic railroad. A group of railroad preservationists is working on that, and another group wants to incorporate the bridge into a rail-trail, which would allow bicyclists to use the bridge. I suppose you could bike across it now on the ties if you have no fear of heights. But I'll pass on that.

After coasting down to the Blackburn Bridge, you shouldn't be surprised to find a stiff climb out of the gorge on the Woodford County side. The toughest part comes early, and the hill tops out at mile 56.5.

60.0 Pass a local park.
Turn left here if you want to visit the Bluegrass Railroad Museum. You can see the museum's restored rail cars from the road.

61.3 Right on Rose Hill Avenue in Versailles, the Woodford County seat.
The town is named for the famous French city, but don't pronounce it as the French do unless you want to be branded as a tourist. The locals say "ver-sales." Just don't forget to switch back if you ever visit France.

Pass the Rose Hill Inn Bed & Breakfast (859-873-5957) a few blocks down.

61.6 Left on Main Street.
Downtown Versailles is just ahead, with several restaurants.

61.7 Right on Lexington Street (US 60 Business).

62.6 Straight as US 60 Bypass comes in from the left.
The road ahead is a two-lane divided highway with paved shoulders. You are now in the heart of Versailles's main shopping district. Within a couple of blocks you can find fast food, slow food, and a big supermarket.

A bike path starts at mile 62.8 and runs to 63.8. After riding roads all the way from Louisville, you may find US 60's wide shoulder as appealing as the bike path.

64.5 Cross under the Blue Grass Parkway.

65.1 Pass a doughnut shop and three convenience stores.

65.5 Pass the Castle Hill Winery.
A few hundred yards past the winery is the castle itself (see Ride 19 for a description).

66.3 Enter Fayette County.

66.7 Pass the Keenelodge Motor Inn (859-254-6699), next to a small store.

68.9 Pass the entrance to Keeneland Race Course.

69.5 Cross Man O War Boulevard.
Many Lexington streets are named for famous horses, and there's no horse more famous than Man O War. He entered 21 races in 1919 and 1920, winning 20 of them, mostly by huge margins. Twice he raced at odds of 1 to 100, which is as close as horseracing comes to a sure thing.

A right turn here would take you the Lexington airport. Some airports are tricky to reach by bike, but this one is easy.

71.0 Cross under New Circle Road (KY 4).

71.8 End at the intersection of Versailles Road (US 60) and Alexandria Drive.
Here you can catch the Number 4 city bus. Or you can keep riding down Versailles Road into the city.

Bicycle Shops

Adrenaline Zone, 614 East Washington Street, Louisville; 502-595-6655

Bardstown Road Bicycles, 1051 Bardstown Road, Louisville; 502-485-9795

Bicycle Sport, 128 Breckenridge Lane, Louisville; 502-897-2611

City BMX, 743 East Washington Street, Louisville; 502-561-0269

Dixie Schwinn, 1803 Rockford Lane, Louisville (in the Shively suburb); 502-448-3448

Highland Cycle, 1737 Bardstown Road, Louisville; 502-458-7832

St. Matthews Schwinn, 106 Sears Avenue, Louisville; 502-895-0553

Scheller's, 11520 Shelbyville Road, Louisville (in the Middletown suburb); 502-245-1955

Scheller's, 8323 Preston Highway, Louisville (in the Okolona suburb); 502-969-4100

Dodds Cyclery, 1985 Harrodsburg Road, Lexington; 859-277-6013

Pedal Power, 401 South Upper Street, Lexington; 859-255-6408

Scheller's, 212 Woodland Avenue, Lexington; 859-233-1764

Vicious Cycle, Todds Road at Codell, Lexington; 859-263-7300

Lodging

Louisville and Lexington have hotels and motels of every kind. If you want to stay overnight on the way, camp at Taylorsville Lake State Park (mile 26.9) or try the Eagle's Motel (502-477-8226) next to the Lakeside Restaurant (mile 20.1).

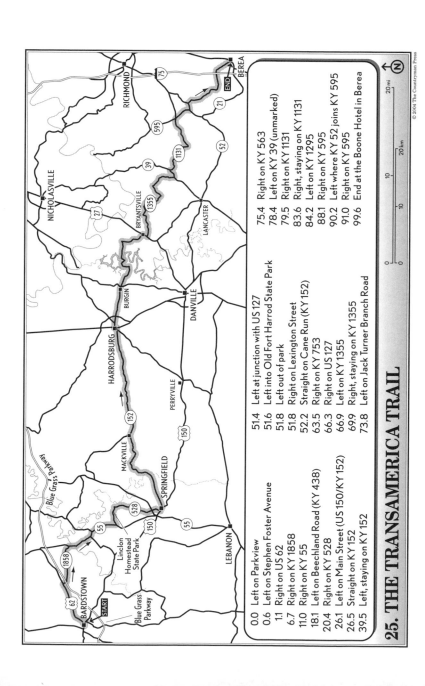

25. THE TRANSAMERICA TRAIL

© 2004 The Countryman Press

0.0	Left on Parkview
0.6	Left on Stephen Foster Avenue
1.1	Right on US 62
6.7	Right on KY 1858
11.0	Right on KY 55
18.1	Left on Beechland Road (KY 438)
20.4	Right on KY 528
26.1	Left on Main Street (US 150/KY 152)
26.5	Straight on KY 152
39.5	Left, staying on KY 152
51.4	Left at junction with US 127
51.6	Left into Old Fort Harrod State Park
51.8	Left out of park
51.8	Right on Lexington Street
52.2	Straight on Cane Run (KY 152)
63.5	Right on KY 753
66.3	Right on US 127
66.9	Left on KY 1355
69.9	Right, staying on KY 1355
73.8	Left on Jack Turner Branch Road
75.4	Right on KY 563
78.4	Left on KY 39 (unmarked)
79.5	Right on KY 1131
83.6	Right, staying on KY 1131
84.2	Left on KY 1295
88.1	Right on KY 595
90.2	Left where KY 52 joins KY 595
91.0	Right on KY 595
99.6	End at the Boone Hotel in Berea

25

The TransAmerica Trail

- **DISTANCE:** 99.6 miles
- **HIGHLIGHTS:** Bardstown and Berea, three state parks, and the chance to ride part of the TransAmerica Trail, a coast-to-coast bike route

People have been biking across the United States for a long time. Thomas Stevens did it in 1884, and went on to bike around the world. Thousands have made the trip since then, following many different routes. Transcontinental cycling became more organized and a lot more popular in the 1970s. The story involves the American Bicentennial and an epic north–south trip.

In 1973 four cyclists—Dan and Lys Burden and Greg and June Siple—were crossing Mexico on their way from Alaska to Argentina. Passing through the town of Chocolate, Greg came up with an idea. To celebrate the 200th anniversary of the Declaration of Independence they would organize a mass crossing of the United States by bicycle. The four travelers followed through on Greg's plan. With the help of other cyclists, they mapped out a route from Oregon to Virginia. They called it the Bikecentennial Trail, and over 2,000 people rode it coast to coast in 1976. The riders came from every state and several foreign countries.

The American Bicentennial came and went, but people kept on riding the Bikecentennial Trail. Eventually, the sponsoring organization changed its name to the Adventure Cycling Association, and the famous route became known as the TransAmerica Trail. Today the association sells maps and guides for several long-distance touring routes, including three that cross the United States. But the favorite route remains the TransAmerica.

This is not a bike path, but a route that follows normal roads, just like most of the tours in this book. And on its way across America it passes through the Bluegrass region. Kentucky can claim over 500 miles of the TransAmerica Trail, and a little more than a fifth of that lies in the Bluegrass. The tour described here covers the 100-mile stretch between Bardstown and Berea. When Donna Lynn Ikenberry wrote *Bicycling Coast to Coast* about her trip on the TransAmerica Trail, she reported that one of her best days occurred on this part of the trail.

The route passes through all three of the Bluegrass subregions. It starts in the open farm country of the Outer Bluegrass, crosses the hilly Eden Shale Belt, and enters the relatively smooth Inner Bluegrass. Then it heads back into the Shale Belt, which surrounds the Inner Bluegrass.

This ride is almost exactly 100 miles long—the cyclist's traditional century ride. You probably think I contrived to make it that length, but I swear I did not. I knew it would be about 100 miles long, but to me that meant anything between 90 and 110. When I scouted the route for this book, I was stunned to see 100.0 on my cyclometer as I pulled up to the Boone Hotel. However, I had detoured to see the Kentucky Artisan Center near Berea, and after deducting this short side trip my mileage was 99.6. But that still rounds to 100.

You can ride this tour in one day if you want the challenge of covering 100 miles in a day. Let me warn you, though, that it is not the easiest century around. It has some hills, and the worst of them come in the second half. If you prefer a more leisurely ride, with time to see the sights along the way, you can easily stretch it out to two or three days, camping or staying in motels along the way.

If you can complete this tour, whether it takes you one day or three, you can ride the whole TransAmerica Trail. You just have to repeat this distance 41 more times. Should you decide to try it, order your maps from the Adventure Cycling Organization (406-721-1776).

DIRECTIONS FOR THE RIDE

Start at the gate to the campground in My Old Kentucky Home State Park. This is the first of three state parks on the tour. The park centers on Federal Hill, a well-preserved mansion from 1818. Supposedly, this is the house that inspired Stephen Foster to write "My Old Kentucky Home," the song that brings tears to the eyes of every true Kentuckian. Some people doubt that story, but in any case it is a lovely house.

0.0 Left on Parkview as you leave the campground.
This road runs along the edge of the state park.

0.6 Left on Stephen Foster Avenue at the T-junction.
The sign says to turn right for Springfield but you need to turn left, even though Springfield is where you are heading. The TransAmerica Trail rarely takes the shortest route; rather, it seeks out the less-traveled back roads.
There are several restaurants nearby.

0.9 Pass the Parkview Motel, with a restaurant next door.

1.1 Right on US 62.
If you go straight instead of right you reach downtown Bardstown in a few blocks. Here you will find one of Kentucky's most interesting churches, the St. Joseph Proto-Cathedral. The "proto" refers to the fact that this used to be a cathedral but is now just a parish church. Built in 1819, it was the first Catholic cathedral in the United States west of the Appalachians. Step inside and you can see gold candlesticks and a collection of huge oil paintings donated by King Louis-Philippe of France. The paintings were stolen once but recovered.

2.0 Cross sharply angled railroad tracks.

2.4 Cross KY 245.
There is a supermarket here, and several smaller stores in the next 2 miles.

3.1 Pass the Down Home Cafe, where the sign reads BREAKFAST FROM 6 AM.

5.1 Pass the Homestead Bed & Breakfast.

6.7 Right on KY 1858.
This is a narrow road with very light traffic. It's a welcome change after moderately busy US 62.

Lincoln Homestead State Park near Springfield.

7.2 Cross over the Blue Grass Parkway.

11.0 Right on KY 55.
The road follows a creek with a series of small waterfalls.

11.7 Cross Beech Fork and enter Washington County.

12.5 Enter the village of Maud.
The country store here closed a long time ago.

15.0 Enter the village of Mooresville (no services).

18.1 Left on Beechland Road (KY 438). A sign points to Lincoln Homestead State Park.

20.4 Reach Lincoln Homestead.
This is the second state park of the tour, with rest rooms and year-round water. The

park has a collection of original and replica log buildings. Honest Abe never lived here, but his ancestors did.

20.4 Right on KY 528.

25.0 Cross KY 555.
This corner supports a fast-food restaurant, two pizza places, a Days Inn, and a supermarket. Stay on KY 528, which is known as Cross Main as you approach downtown Springfield.

26.1 Left on Main Street (US 150 and KY 152).
The courthouse on the corner dates from 1816. It's Kentucky's oldest.

26.4 Pass a supermarket and another pizza place.
This is the last stop for many miles.

26.5 Straight on KY 152 as US 150 splits right.

30.8 Cross Beech Fork.
The route is now crossing the Eden Shale Belt, a region of ridges and V-shaped valleys with less open land than the Outer or Inner Bluegrass.

36.8 Enter Mackville (no services). Stay with KY 152 as it turns right and then left out of town.

39.5 Left at the fork, staying on KY 152 as KY 442 heads off to the right.

40.9 Enter Mercer County.
On the left a rust-covered bicycle wheel with a three-speed hub is nailed to a pole. Is there a message here?

46.8 Pass a country store.

49.7 Cross the Salt River.
There is a picnic area on the west bank (before you cross the bridge). Bike tourists may camp here free if they tell the local police. Such free camping is available in many spots along the TransAmerica Trail.

50.5 Enter Harrodsburg on Mooreland Avenue.
This is the oldest continuously inhabited community in Kentucky. Unlike Boonesborough, that other very early settlement, Harrodsburg thrived and has turned into a prosperous, modern town.

51.2 Straight as US 68 comes in from the right and joins KY 152.

51.4 Left at the US 127 junction. US 68, US 127, and KY 152 all run together here.

51.6 Left into Old Fort Harrod State Park, the third state park of the tour.
The Harrodstown Motel and the Parkview Guest House are just outside the park entrance. The park contains a replica of the old fort, a small museum, and the Lincoln Marriage Temple, a church-like stone structure that encloses the log house in which Abraham Lincoln's parents were married. That's all very nice, but my favorite part of the park is the huge Osage orange tree, split by lightning but still alive.

51.8 Left on leaving the park, then right on Lexington Street. US 68 and KY 152 make the turn with you, while US 127 continues north.

51.9 Cross Main Street.
Downtown Harrodsburg, with a restaurant or two, is to your right.

52.1 Cross railroad tracks.

52.2 Straight on Cane Run as US 68 and most of the traffic split left. Stay on KY 152.

53.1 Cross US 127 Bypass and say good-bye to Harrodsburg.

56.2 Cross railroad tracks as you reach the center of Burgin, which has a small grocery store.

56.6 Cross KY 33.
There is a small restaurant at the corner. If you detour to the left you'll find a store a short way down 33.

61.0 Cross Herrington Lake on the Kennedy Bridge and enter Garrard (rhymes with "Jared") County.
A left turn just before the bridge would take you to the Chimney Rock Campground.
   Herrington Lake was formed by damming the Dix River, which flows into the Kentucky River near the High Bridge. When finished in 1927, the Dix Dam was the world's biggest rock-filled dam. Unlike most Kentucky dams, which were built for flood control and recreation, this one was made to generate electricity. The lake is

narrow because the Dix River used to run through a deep gorge. The gorge is still there, but most of it is now under water.

61.4 Pass a store.

63.5 Right on KY 753 at Buena Vista, which has a small store.

66.3 Right on US 127.
This is a busy two-lane highway, and no fun to ride. But you're on it for less than a mile.

66.9 Left on KY 1355.
There is a convenience store on the corner.

69.9 Right at the fork to stay on KY 1355.

73.3 Cross Sugar Creek at Three Forks.
The West, Middle, and East Forks of Sugar Creek come together here.

73.8 Left on Jack Turner Branch Road. It's marked but easy to miss, so keep an eye peeled as you approach.
Though less than 2 miles long, this road is a treat. It's one lane wide and goes through the woods, sticking close to the creek for which it was named. It climbs all the way, but the grade is mild except for the last few yards.

75.4 Right on KY 563 at a T-junction.

78.4 Left on KY 39 (unmarked).

79.5 Right on KY 1131 in the village of McCreary, which has a country store.

83.6 Right to stay on KY 1131.

84.2 Left on KY 1295 at a T-junction.

86.7 Enter Madison County and start a climb.

88.1 Right on KY 595.
There are some turns ahead, but 595 will see you all the way to your destination.

90.2 Left at a T-junction as KY 52 joins KY 595.

91.0 Right on KY 595 as KY 52 goes its own way.
The village here is called Happy Landing, and has a country store.

At mile 91.5, look right for a good example of a cane field. Kentucky cane is a grass that resembles bamboo. Early settlers found it all over the Bluegrass, but you have to look for it these days.

97.1 Cross under I-75.
You are at Exit 77, which has convenience stores, two motels, and a steak house. Just past I-75 you'll find the big new Kentucky Artisan Center and Cafe. The Beebe-White Bikeway starts here and provides an alternate route into Berea. The bike path runs next to KY 595.

98.0 Cross angled railroad tracks.

99.6 End in downtown Berea at the Boone Hotel.

Bicycle Shops

Bikes N Bargains, 1440 East John Rowan Boulevard, Bardstown; 502-348-4096

Lodging

Bardstown, Springfield, Harrodsburg, and Berea all have motels right on the route. You can find a room close to the start point at the Parkview Motel (502-348-5983) on Stephen Foster Avenue in Bardstown. The Boone Hotel (859-985-3700) at the end of the ride is another good choice. Camping is available in My Old Kentucky Home State Park at the start point and at the Chimney Rock Campground near mile 61. Berea has two commercial campgrounds, both located off the route on the west side of town.

RESOURCES Here are some books you may find helpful in planning your Bluegrass bike trips:

- *The WPA Guide to Kentucky*, first published in 1939 and republished in 1996. It's old, but nothing written since can match it.
- *Kentucky Off the Beaten Path*, by Zoè Ann Stecker.
- *Country Roads of Kentucky*, by Mary Augusta Rodgers.
- *Wheeling Around the Bluegrass*, by Joe Ward.
- *Cyclin' the Blue Grass*, by John A. Deacon. This book is out of print, but some libraries have it.

Even the best guidebooks cannot replace maps. Ordinary road maps are useful, but they lack the detail that bicyclists sometimes need. Here are two good map collections:

- *Kentucky Atlas and Gazetteer*, one of the DeLorme series of state atlases. It shows just about every road in the state, along with elevation contour lines and details on campgrounds, parks, and points of interest. Unfortunately, the atlas does not distinguish public from private roads. More than once I've tried to get through on a minor road and found it gated and locked.
- *Kentucky County Maps*, edited by C. J Puetz. It's not as fancy as the DeLorme atlas, but it shows all the public roads and notes which ones are paved.

Cycling clubs offer group rides and information about local conditions. The Bluegrass region has two:

Bluegrass Cycling Club
P.O. Box 1397
Lexington, KY 40588
www.bgcycling.org

Louisville Bicycle Club
P.O. Box 35541
Louisville, KY 40232
www.louisvillebicycleclub.org

Index

Let Countryman Take You There

Our experienced authors will lead you to the finest trails, parks, and back roads in the following areas:

50 Hikes Series
50 Hikes in the Adirondacks
50 Hikes in Colorado
50 Hikes in Connecticut
50 Hikes in Central Florida
50 Hikes in North Florida
50 Hikes in South Florida
50 Hikes in the Lower Hudson Valley
50 Hikes in Kentucky
50 Hikes in the Maine Mountains
50 Hikes in Coastal and Southern Maine
50 Hikes in Louisiana
50 Hikes in Massachusetts
50 Hikes in Maryland
50 Hikes in Michigan
50 Hikes in the White Mountains
50 More Hikes in New Hampshire
50 Hikes in New Jersey
50 Hikes in Central New York
50 Hikes in Western New York
50 Hikes in the Mountains of North Carolina
50 Hikes in Ohio
50 More Hikes in Ohio
50 Hikes in Eastern Pennsylvania
50 Hikes in Central Pennsylvania
50 Hikes in Western Pennsylvania
50 Hikes in the Tennessee Mountains
50 Hikes in Vermont
50 Hikes in Northern Virginia
50 Hikes in Southern Virginia
50 Hikes in Wisconsin

Walking
Hikes & Walks in the Berkshire Hills
Walks and Rambles on Cape Cod and the Islands
Walks and Rambles on the Delmarva Peninsula
Walks and Rambles in the Western Hudson Valley
Walks and Rambles on Long Island
Walks and Rambles in Ohio's Western Reserve
Walks and Rambles in Rhode Island
Walks and Rambles in and around St. Louis
Weekend Walks in St. Louis and Beyond
Weekend Walks Along the New England Coast
Weekend Walks in Historic New England
Weekend Walks in the Historic Washington D.C. Region

Bicycling
25 Bicycle Tours in the Adirondacks
25 Bicycle Tours on Delmarva
25 Bicycle Tours in Savannah and the Carolina Low Country
25 Bicycle Tours in Maine
25 Bicycle Tours in Maryland
25 Bicycle Tours in the Twin Cities and Southeastern Minnesota
30 Bicycle Tours in New Jersey
25 Bicycle Tours in the Hudson Valley
25 Bicycle Tours in the Lake Champlain Region
25 Bicycle Tours in Maryland
25 Bicycle Tours in Ohio's Western Reserve
25 Bicycle Tours in the Texas Hill Country and West Texas
25 Bicycle Tours in Vermont
25 Bicycle Tours in and around Washington, D.C.
25 Mountain Bike Tours in the Adirondacks
25 Mountain Bike Tours in the Hudson Valley
25 Mountain Bike Tours in Massachusetts
25 Mountain Bike Tours in New Jersey
Backroad Bicycling in the Blue Ridge and Smoky Mountains
Backroad Bicycling in Connecticut
Backroad Bicycling on Cape Cod, Martha's Vineyard, and Nantucket
Backroad Bicycling in the Finger Lakes Region
Backroad Bicycling in Western Massachusetts
Backroad Bicycling in New Hampshire
Backroad Bicycling in Eastern Pennsylvania
Backroad Bicycling in Wisconsin
The Mountain Biker's Guide to Ski Resorts
Bicycling America's National Parks: Arizona & New Mexico
Bicycling America's National Parks: California
Bicycling America's National Parks: Oregon & Washington
Bicycling America's National Parks: Utah & Colorado
Bicycling Cuba

We offer many more books on hiking, fly-fishing, travel, nature, and other subjects. Our books are available at bookstores and outdoor stores everywhere. For more information or a free catalog, please call 1-800-245-4151 or write to us at The Countryman Press, P.O. Box 748, Woodstock, Vermont 05091. You can find us online at www.countrymanpress.com.